The Chronicles of

NOAH
AND HER SISTERS

The Chronicles of

NOAH

AND HER SISTERS

Genesis and Exodus According to Women

Miriam Therese Winter

Illustrations by Eunice Cudzewicz

CROSSROAD • NEW YORK

1995

The Crossroad Publishing Company
370 Lexington Avenue, New York, NY 10017

Copyright © 1995 by Medical Mission Sisters

Printed in the United States of America

Library of Congress Cataloging-in-Publication Data

Winter, Miriam Therese.
    The chronicles of Noah and her sisters : Genesis and Exodus
according to women / Miriam Therese Winter.
        p.   cm.
    ISBN 0-8245-1509-9 (pbk.)
    1. Bible. O.T. Genesis—History of Biblical events—Fiction.
2. Bible. O.T. Exodus—History of Biblical events—Fiction.
3. Women in the Bible—Fiction.   I. Title.
PS3573.I538C48   1995
813'.54—dc20   95-18594
                                                        CIP

CONTENTS

LIST OF ILLUSTRATIONS

Cover design and text illustrations by Eunice Cudzewicz. Eunice, a Medical Mission Sister, is director of the community's global communications and editor of *Intercontinent*. She resides in Philadelphia.

INTRODUCTION

When we teach the Bible to children, we step right into the story to make it come alive, spinning a tale of fantasy and fact in ways that stir the imagination and captivate the heart. Images molded by troubadours and bards, and preschool religion teachers, remain with us forever, like the singsong parade of animals moving forward, two by two, into a lopsided ark.

Knowing which part of the text can be attributed to the Yahwist's record and which to the Elohist source cannot quite match the impact of the storyteller's tale. Certainly, scholarship is vital to the integrity of texts. The study of a text, however, is different from its celebration. Too often we tend to get stuck in our heads during our rites and rituals, so our words seldom sing in our hearts. We present biblical narratives in ways that distance us from them and, too often, mystify. Instead of life touching life, as past and present meet and merge, our usual liturgies of the word are all about hearing a biblical text proclaimed and interpreted and are not a reality shared.

Those among us who continue to turn to the biblical narratives as core to our celebrations, if only from time to time, seek a more direct access to their underlying storyline. In order to connect life now in meaningful relationship to biblical antiquity, we need to be able to bypass the complex layers of application and interpretation within the canon. This is essential for women who, for countless generations, have absorbed and internalized the message of female degradation encoded in patriarchal texts. *The Chronicles of Noah and Her Sisters* is a retelling of the stories of Genesis and Exodus according to the perspective of women. The book is a blend of familiar tales told with improvisation. It is written with the conviction that the world of once-upon-a-time can be as valid as the really real.

The Noah of the Chronicles

Solomon, son of David, had one thousand wives, so the Scriptures tell us. This statistic may be exaggerated, but it is a biblical fact. Seven hundred of the women were princesses; three hundred were concubines (1 Kings 11:3). Only Naamah, mother of Rehoboam, the son who succeeded Solomon to reign over Judah, is identified by name (2 Chr 12:13). Solomon married both for love and for political expediency. He wed Moabite, Ammonite, Edomite, Hittite, Sidonian, and Egyptian women in a diplomatic effort to establish a formidable empire, since marrying the daughters and sisters of kings would effectively seal alliances favorable to commerce and peace.

It is safe to assume that Solomon also married Hebrew women. Here, where we depart from Scripture, is where our story begins. One of Solomon's Hebrew wives was a gifted storyteller who had taught herself to read and write with the help of a palace scribe. The woman's name was Noah. She was the one who would gather the women within the royal harem anytime there was an occasion for cultic festivity. She had a feel for history and an affinity for tradition. Due to her tireless efforts, circles of Hebrew women met within the palace quarters to share their stories and to transmit their collective memories to their daughters and female friends.

Noah knew the creation myths at the heart of other traditions, for she shared in all the rituals arising from the spiritual diversity embraced by Solomon's wives. She knew best of all those foundational stories of the Israelite tradition, including the versions told by women in circles of their own. She was aware that the central narratives that shaped tradition in Judah differed from similar accounts that had long been popular in the north. She had seen some stories that had been written down and knew the authorities were apprehensive concerning conflicting accounts. She too was anxious, but for reasons other than north-south variations. Tradition was understood differently by Hebrew women and men, and the patriarchal structures seemed to be taking male interpretation as normative for all.

Noah gathered all the stories told by the Hebrew women who met to remember with her, compared them with what she herself had heard when she was a girl at home, and wrote her own account. Her chronicles circulated among the women for several generations before they disappeared. It was said that just before Jerusalem fell and prior to its invasion, a woman dug a hole in the ground and buried the scrolls of Noah. Recently, they were unearthed during excavations along the outer wall and painstakingly translated. Genesis and Exodus according to women are published for the first time in their entirety here.

There are three women named Noah associated with these chronicles. Noah, wife of Solomon, the author of this apocryphal account, exists only in our imagination. Her link to another Noah, whose story is essential here, is also fictional, although the woman herself is real. Noah the author traces her lineage back through her great grandmother to the Noah of the exodus, one of five sisters known as the daughters of Zelophehad in the canonical texts (Num 27:1–11). The Bible identifies Noah and her sisters by name. The third Noah, hero of the Genesis myth of flood, ark, and rainbow, is a wisdom figure for the other two and paradigmatic for us all.

The Chronicles of Noah and Her Sisters reflects the spirit of the Noah of Genesis, the Noah of the exodus, and the Noah of the court of Solomon, and celebrates all three women, each in a different way.

The Chronicles of Noah

Throughout these chronicles of Noah, traditional biblical narratives are presented in a midrashic mode.

Midrash, a homiletic commentary on the Hebrew Scriptures, is a Jewish method of interpretation that goes beyond the obvious meaning of a biblical passage in search of more elusive implications. Often highly imaginative, this approach makes use of allegory and legend in order to probe the Scriptures for the wisdom within. One always begins with the canonical text, but one is free to move beyond it. *The Chronicles of Noah and Her Sisters* is an attempt at Christian midrash based on two books of the Hebrew Scriptures that are part of the Christian canon.

In the spirit and style of midrash, these chronicles offer a journey through tradition, interrupted by surprise. The starting point is the biblical text, so the stories and themes are familiar, but then imagination, or perhaps intuition, invites us beyond the words on the page into an experience of what might have been and is no longer remembered.

The opening chapters of Genesis are presented as cultural myths, and what follows, as cultural traditions. In this book, as in the Bible, there is no clear distinction between myth and historical account, although myths seem to encourage a more imaginative reconstruction. Without doubt there are mythical materials in the historical narratives and, conversely, something of historical fact underlying cultural myths. It is inaccurate to say that one is true and the other is not, for both myth and history deal with truth, but from totally different perspectives. Universal truths are embedded in mythic tales and epic ventures, and there are times when we come closer to truth by encountering a myth. Joseph Campbell, in *The Power of Myth*, says that myths are "stories about the wisdom of life" (p. 9). The purpose of *The Chronicles of Noah and Her Sisters* is to put those of us who enter into these tales in touch with the wisdom of life.

These chronicles give voice and visibility to women in biblical tradition. The approach is feminist, a term meant to be inclusive of both women and men. Men as well as women have come to realize the androcentric nature of our canonical Scriptures and the patriarchal bias that has pushed women to the margins and, at times, out of the Book. Familiar events are revisited through an intuitive understanding and the prism of women's experience, which reflects things differently. Once we have put on a feminist lens and honored women's perspective, it is easier to imagine how some events might have happened another way.

The myths are those opening narratives from the account of creation through the episode of the tower. With the appearance of Sarah and Abraham, real people with a history and a future step onto the stage of life. Storytellers resist revealing details of a plot prior to its performance. Nevertheless, the following notes are offered, not as grist for analysis, but as a brief introduction to an imaginative reinterpretation of some of the best loved tales of our religious tradition.

In the beginning S/HE Who Is imagines a universe. The One Who, from the beginning, is within and beyond all that has life creates our planet earth and its inhabitants. The story of the birth of humanity is prior to the story of Eden.

The garden narrative is no longer a creation myth, but a story of relationship. The juxtaposition of wild and tame, female and male, and different ways of relating to God and to creation is a part of paradise, as it is of ordinary life. This means that women who hear this story can enter and leave the garden without patriarchal baggage, and little girls who approach the tree of life can grow up feeling good about themselves. To be who God created us to be, wise and understanding, is seen as essential to living, as a choice in our struggle to be fully human. Intimacy with the "other," with whoever or whatever is different from ourselves, is at the heart of the story. Adam and Eve do not fall into sin. They simply fall in love, an outcome intrinsically human that, in the beginning, is very good. Woven into the narrative are italicized phrases from the Song of Songs, that sensual, mystical, canonical book that also features a woman and a man, a garden and an apple tree, and the dynamics of love.

The legend of the flood is common to many cultures and religions around the world where, consistently, the hero is male. It would seem that women participating in the telling of this tale might present it a different way, with one of their own as protagonist, for innovation and imagination, tools of the storyteller's craft, are gifts of both women and men. Therefore, the chronicles introduce Noah, not the man but the woman, as central to the myth. The covenant signified by the rainbow marks her solemn commitment to live intimately interconnected to all living things. It is important to remember that the first covenant God initiates in the Bible is the covenant with Noah on behalf of all creation. Responsibility for safeguarding life on this planet in all of its manifestations is, therefore, biblically based. One cannot possibly have dominion over any living species when one is living in solidarity and in harmony with all of life.

If Sarah had kept a diary, we would have had to speculate less. Instead, her story has come down to us through channels far removed from Sarah's circle of experience. Since much of the material in authoritative texts is already imaginative, it seemed quite natural to seek to weave a wider scenario, particularly when one admits up front that her story is just that, a story, and not autobiography.

Sarah is a compelling figure, a quintessential matriarch whose influence has been diminished in traditional accounts. There is so much more to Sarah than we have been led to believe, as indicated by traces of information within the Genesis texts. She may have been a Mesopotamian sage, perhaps even a priestess, as Savina Teubal insists in her study *Sarah the Priestess*. She certainly was a woman of authority in the sphere of her influence. In *The Chronicles of Noah and Her Sisters,* new aspects of her relationship with Hagar are explored. Hagar, herself a women of consequence in her time and our own, is shown to be more than a victim. She is a woman of heroic stature, and the child of her womb is rightfully recognized as heir to the blessings of God.

The enigmatic Keturah, whom the Bible says gave Abraham six sons after the death of Sarah, emerges from the shadows of the past into a life of her own. To think that Abraham could father six sons after he was well over one hundred years of age strains credibility. However, textual evidence suggests that Abraham's father and his brother Nahor both had dual households and separate families, giving some basis for saying of Abraham, like father, like son.

The narratives of Rebekah, Rachel, and Leah are consistent with the expectations of a matriarchal reality. These giants from an irretrievable past seem far more accessible once we add flesh to the bare bones of biblical biography. We catch a glimpse of their deeds and desires in their relationships to patriarchal men, their husbands and progeny. Throughout his life, the patriarch Jacob is bonded to strong, matriarchal women, first to his mother, Rebekah, then to Rachel, his wife. He honors their legacy in a blessing bestowed on his daughter Dinah, elaborating on a remnant of matriarchal imagery embedded in the Genesis text (49:25-26).

A large part of Genesis, in the Bible and in these chronicles, focuses on the children of Sarah, Rebekah, Rachel, and Leah. All but one are sons. The story of Dinah, Leah's daughter, aborted in its traditional setting, comes alive in this retelling, suggesting she was more than an unfortunate female overshadowed by twelve sibling males. She and another survivor, Tamar, are examples of courage for every woman victimized by abuse. On the other hand, Joseph, the favored son, is shown to have feet of clay. For example, we learn from Potiphar's wife that there may be another side to what transpired between them. Through Asenath, Joseph's Egyptian wife, we encounter the extent of his cultural and religious assimilation and the consequences for his kin. There is indeed a checkered lining to Joseph's technicolor dream coat. Joseph may have been a dreamer, but the aftermath of the famine in Egypt was a nightmare for the Hebrews, who

came out of it enslaved. His ingenuity and largess led to generations of oppression for the Hebrew people and resulted in a
discontinuity between their future and their past.

Exodus follows Genesis in one unbroken story, as sojourners
trapped in an alien land boldly orchestrate their escape, only
to discover in the wilderness how hard it is to go home again
once you have left your home. Moses, who emerges as larger
than life in the canonical narratives, is torn by his insecuri-
ties, his dependence on Miriam and Aaron, and his marriages
to the Cushite woman and to Zipporah the Midianite. Miriam, a
prophet and poet who enjoys the confidence of her people, is a
wellspring of wisdom, especially for the women. She is a skillful
leader, a risk taker who boldly incarnates the heart and soul of
a people.

The plagues are presented with a new twist, suggesting
human participation in the scourges befalling Pharaoh. Only
seven plagues are reported, which is consistent with earlier
traditions that indicate there were less than ten. The exodus
itself occurs in stages, quietly and unobtrusively, with the Egyptians assisting their beleaguered friends in making their escape,
right up until the final run culminating at the Sea of Reeds.
Clues within the canonical texts support the development of an
alternative script similar to what is presented here.

No attempt is made in this retelling to indicate the length of
time spent in the wilderness, although the main reason offered
for the circuitous route from Egypt to Canaan may well be ac-
curate. Noah, Zelophehad's daughter, provides a serendipitous
moment of winsomeness and wisdom out in the wilderness.
Noah, like her namesake, is clearly a channel for S/HE Who
Is. Her embodied spirituality enables us to connect to that
covenant made by the mythical Noah in solidarity with all
creation, and to embrace it as our own.

As the exodus story draws to a close with the men poised to
enter Canaan forcefully, if necessary, over the objections of the
women, we anticipate the helplessness of the faithful female
remnant. Surely, what will follow is the suppression of S/HE

Who Is. All is irrevocably lost, says logic, but the heart knows otherwise, for Noah keeps the memory alive until it is safe for it to surface with its liberating power. The intuitive wisdom inherent in her, which links past to present, spirals forward to encircle us. As the chronicles end, we are confident that S/HE Who Is lives on.

Central Themes of Genesis and Exodus According to Women

One of the aims of *The Chronicles of Noah and Her Sisters* has been to image and name God within biblical tradition in ways acceptable to both women and men. To do this, it was necessary to emphasize the matriarchal contexts behind the received texts and to reveal the integral connection between women, who are bearers of life, and all life within creation. These three distinct yet related realities, namely, relationship with God, matriarchal traditions, and concern for all creation are the central themes of the chronicles. These themes are based on material indigenous to the Genesis and Exodus books within the biblical canon. A brief commentary on these themes will give some indication of how they have been developed here.

We who are created in the image of God can see ourselves as imaging God when image is congruent with name. Therefore, in the chronicles, the primary name for God is S/HE. This pronoun, consisting of female and male as distinct and yet as one, is a name used by women and men. However, S/HE is perceived differently by women and by men. Two different words have been used to indicate these diverse perceptions. "Godde" reflects the understanding of women. "God" represents the perspective of men. As women enter into relationship with Godde, they name the Godde of their experience. S/HE Who Is, Shekinah, Shaddai are names favored by the women. Men also name their encounters with God. Before the name YHWH becomes prevalent, men prefer El Shaddai and El Olam.

Studies confirm that goddess civilizations flourished for many thousands of years up to and into biblical times. Numerous figurines unearthed around the world attest to the preeminence of female deities in prehistoric societies, and scholars continue to shed new light on the distinct and multiple mythologies underlying goddess religions and their influential cults. The goddess Asherah was popular in Canaan and in Egypt. Her female spirit was believed to be present in a fruit-bearing tree or a leafy tree, and her symbol was the "tree of life." Her sanctuary was said to be a grove of trees similar to the one where Sarah settled. Some goddesses, such as Asherah, and the closely related Astarte of Syria and Ishtar of Babylonia, were culturally distinct aspects of a common myth. Most likely, others were manifestations of multiple deities.

The earliest traditions of Genesis and Exodus evolved within this religious environment. The veneration of Asherah seems to have been a tradition among the women of Genesis. It was definitely part of Israel's cultic practice in succeeding generations, according to references in Deuteronomy, Judges, and both books of Kings. Exactly how Asherah was perceived by women within biblical tradition is a point to be debated. In this retelling of Genesis and Exodus, Asherah is an aspect of Godde, yet there is only one God, for God/de is one. The Godde of Hebrew women is the God of Hebrew men, understood differently perhaps, but nevertheless the same. S/HE of multiple manifestations and often conflicting theologies is known by many names.

Matriarchal societies were the norm in goddess civilizations. The matriarchs of Genesis struggled to assure the continuity of their ancient traditions, even as they were embracing a changing way of life. The households of Sarah and Rebekah were matrilinear and matrilocal. Sons were sent to their mother's family to seek and secure a wife. Although we assume the primacy of the firstborn in biblical tradition, this patriarchal principle was slow in taking root. The younger child is the child of choice in Genesis and Exodus. This is a matriarchal practice.

Abel, Cain's younger brother, was favored. Isaac was Abraham's second son. Jacob was younger than Esau. Judah, heir to the covenant, and Joseph, the one who outwitted the famine, were Jacob's younger sons. Rachel, whom Jacob loved best of all, was younger than her sister, Leah. Ephraim, Joseph's secondborn, received Jacob's special blessing. Moses, liberator of his people, was Miriam's baby brother. Clearly, Scripture reveals to us that those favored by God and tradition were not always firstborn sons, despite all the rhetoric.

The Chronicles of Noah and Her Sisters takes these perspectives and builds on them in ways that differ from the norm, all the while affirming the importance of women and the contributions of the matriarchs. Legendary women, strong and confident, shape these narratives. They take charge and lead, acting decisively, sometimes deceitfully in order to accomplish their objectives. An intriguing secondary theme features Rachel's *teraphim,* which she supposedly stole from her father, who insisted that they were his household gods (Gen 31:19, 30). These sacred or ritual objects seem to assume a tradition of their own, witnessing to the tenacity of women's rituals and women's ways.

The third theme central to this imaginative reconstruction emerges in the beginning with the formation of the universe and the evolution of planet earth. Creation itself is precious. All creation, all that has life is universal blessing. This perspective rejects unequivocally the charge to have dominion over any person or any living thing. The temptation to subjugate and subdue violates the integrity of the web of life. Ancient civilizations understood this, for Gaia was once a name for both the deity and planet earth. Riane Eisler in *The Chalice and the Blade* writes convincingly of the non-dominator model of partnership societies prior to the invasion of patriarchal tribes and the destruction of a peaceful way of life. There was a time, so we are told, when prehistoric societies lived in wholistic harmony with earth and the forces of the universe. These chronicles capture that ancient spirit in the ethos of the women, who enter into earth rituals honoring its cycles and its seasons, and vow to live in peace.

Tensions between matriarchal assumptions and patriarchal alternatives create a counterpoint to the central themes. Diverse worldviews converge and clash, and one will ultimately dominate, but not yet, not in these chronicles, which originate in once upon a time. In *The Chronicles of Noah and Her Sisters,* women "get it," men get what they want, and both seem reasonably satisfied. But then, myths are not the end of the story; they are only the beginning. We who enter into the myth must reaffirm, reinterpret, or reinvent all along its storyline.

In their book *Hebrew Myths: The Book of Genesis,* Robert Graves and Raphael Patai write: "Myths are dramatic stories that form a sacred charter either authorizing the continuance of ancient institutions, customs, rites and beliefs in the area where they are current, or approving alterations" (p. 11). Much power has been attributed to myths, power to influence individuals and groups, power to shape and sustain institutions and institutionalized behaviors, whether good or bad. Scriptures, comprising myth and mythic materials interwoven with religious and historical fact, are repositories of dominator attitudes, of political and theological bias from the perspective of those on top. It is necessary not only to demythologize but to re-mythologize biblical narratives in order to access and liberate the wealth of wisdom material forced to conform to the limits of texts. Harold Bloom writes in *The Book of J:*

> Few cultural paradoxes are so profound, or so unnerving, as the process of religious canonization by which an essentially literary work becomes a sacred text. When script becomes Scripture, reading is numbed by taboo and inhibition. Even if imagining an author and calling her J is an arbitrary and personal fiction, something like that is necessary if we are to be stirred out of our numbness. (p. 35)

Bloom suggests that the Yahwist account was written by a woman and that it reflects women's experience within biblical tradition. Even if the fact cannot be confirmed, even if a female author cannot be found, he believes it is legitimate to invent one.

These chronicles take Bloom's words to heart. Through Noah, a literary invention, Genesis and Exodus come to life in ways that validate women. *The Chronicles of Noah and Her Sisters* is a retelling of the story of the origins of our religious tradition from the perspective of the women at the heart of the narratives. It is meant to inspire and affirm women for whom these stories are Scripture. It is meant to inspire and enlighten men accustomed to other interpretations. It is meant to show that our ancient stories can be revelatory for our times and transformative for us all.

What follows is both fact and fiction, and neither fact nor fiction. It is simply the story of a people, particularly their women, written in the style of a testament, not as a replacement for the biblical Testament, but as an alternative text for the appropriate occasions. While recommended for personal spiritual reading and other private practices, it is primarily intended for ritual use and is written to be read aloud.

Alternative communities of faith and feminist spirituality who are assembling to celebrate Wisdom and Word and to embrace the process of appropriation so integral to the Bible are characteristic of our times. They are continuing the tradition of interpretation and integration, whether or not they know it. They are also birthing their own rich, unrecorded traditions similar to those that underlie authoritative texts. This process, which for centuries was a vital part of liturgical celebration, lives again in storytelling, theologizing communities and groups, particularly those of women. Here is a text for communities such as these who gather to celebrate life.

Story is and has always been central to liturgy, and liturgy is essentially life. Through liturgy and through ritual, we reenact, relive, remember that which is vital for us to know. Liturgy monitors the pulse of our spiritual well-being. Authentic liturgy helps us understand spirituality, not as something unrelated to

life or something we decide to do when we have time or incli-
nation, but as life itself made more fully alive through rituals of
the spirit.

May all who turn to these chronicles to facilitate a spiritual
renewal and to seek to live justly for the sake of all on earth
receive from the experience enough wisdom for the journey,
enough hope for continuing on.

Acknowledgments

I have always had a love for maps. Before embarking on this
literary journey, I spent hours mapping itineraries and routes
and studying the geographical relationships between the villages I would be visiting and the countries they were in. I
also spent time charting genealogies from the perspective of
the matriarchs, grateful for my prior work with the women of
the Hebrew Scriptures in *WomanWisdom* and *WomanWitness*. I
reached back into experience and called upon my months in Israel and my weeks in the Sinai desert. As a result of having been
there myself, I could accompany the women on their journey,
feel the intensity of the scorching sun, understand the gut-level
meaning of water when one's whole being is racked with thirst.
I could see and taste the bubbling spring, visualize the oasis
of Paran, feel the fronds of its palms refresh my body and my
spirit. I knew every step to the top of Mount Sinai, for I too
had climbed the mountain three different times. Exodus took
me back to the future, just as these stories were meant to do in
every generation. I was caught up in the power of the narratives,
even as they were being born again.

I am grateful to the scholars who wrote all the books and ar-
ticles I read and authors whom only those scholars have read.
My understanding of biblical sources and goddess civilizations I
owe directly to them. I would like to thank Arthur Waskow for
pointing out the connection between the garden story of Genesis and the Song of Songs in "The Bible's Sleeping Beauty and

Her Great-Granddaughters" (*Tikkun* 4 [March–April 1989]: 126–28), and Elizabeth A. Johnson for the gift of *She Who Is: The Mystery of God in Feminist Discourse* (1993). Thanks also to Savina J. Teubal for her insights and her scholarship in both *Sarah the Priestess: The First Matriarch of Genesis* (1984) and *Hagar the Egyptian: The Lost Tradition of the Matriarchs* (1990).

I am especially grateful to the following people: to Rabbi Ilyse Kramer for reading a draft of the manuscript and for offering sage advice; to Eunice Cudzewicz, a Medical Mission Sister and friend, for her cover art and textual illustrations; to my community of Medical Mission Sisters, especially Mary Elizabeth Johnson, who is in ministry with me, for a graced context in which to grow; to all in the Crossroad Publishing family for encouraging creativity and for being so supportive; and to the UConn Huskies, the women's basketball team of the University of Connecticut, who captured the national championship title and the hearts of the nation as I was finishing these lines. Their story, the stuff that myths are made of, mirrors the heroic prototypes these chronicles remember and shows us what women of integrity can be and become.

Finally, gratitude overflows when I recall how the Spirit and the spirits of the women of Genesis and Exodus inspired and accompanied me. Indeed, it is Godde who enabled the myths and the memories to live again.

To S/HE Who Is, glory be!

The Chronicles of

NOAH
AND HER SISTERS

Genesis and Exodus
According to Women

CULTURAL MYTHS

✧ In the Beginning _____

In the beginning
S/HE:
Shekinah...
Shaddai...
self consisting
self existing
self sustaining
S/HE
All in all
S/HE
eternal Being and Becoming,
One with all that is being and becoming
visible, viable, vulnerable:
Life
giving life,
giving love,
receiving love,
so it is
as it was
in the beginning.
At home in the vast expanse of forever,
Life eternal,
Love everlasting
imagines a world that is wonder full,
filled with abundance
and beauty
and love.
S/HE casts a circle
wide and deep
and dreams a universe.
Pleased by the pull of its planets

and the lure of its galaxies,
S/HE rejoices,
playing with all S/HE has made,
S/HE Who Is
eternally beginning.

✧ Creation of Earth _____

Once upon a time,
in a time before time,
before the mountains had been shaped,
before the valleys ventured forth,
before the stars could blink their eyes,
before sunlight and shadow,
S/HE shuddered, deity in travail
as waters burst from the womb of Life
to fill the empty spaces,
to wash the world S/HE was bringing to birth
and would forever nurture:
moist earth, virgin forests,
seed-bearing plants and colorful flowers
cascading in and out of time
through cycles of energy and rest,
for a time, and times, and half a time.
So it was in the beginning.
S/HE of a thousand names,
S/HE of ten thousand images
created a world S/HE would inhabit,
cradled sun and moon and stars
and rocked to the rhythms of day into night,
winter to spring, time to eternity, singing:
"Good. So very good."

S/HE blew sweet breath to the farthest ends
and laughed as birds flew into the wind
when S/HE lifted two all-encompassing wings.
Caterpillars turning to butterflies,
beetles and bugs that creep and crawl
covered the landscape with fanciful shapes
and symphonies of sound.
Fish filled the waterways.
Frogs and turtles, serpents and snakes,
four-footed creatures large and small
like deer and dog and tiger and bear
and elk and elephant
S/HE made
and played among them,
saying aloud:
"So good. So very good."

Poised at the portals of dawn,
S/HE sang:
"Let us make more life in Our image."
And so S/HE created humankind,
female and male S/HE created us,
light and dark S/HE created us,
every size and shape S/HE created us,
in the image of Love,
with the breath of Life,
in the Spirit of peace S/HE created us,
good, so good S/HE created us,
blessing us, every one.
"Be fruitful," S/HE said.
"Fill the earth with your giftedness
and your goodness.
Multiply your blessings."

Then S/HE whispered into the universe:
"Happy are all who keep My ways,

who seek after wisdom.
Holy are all who are one with all of Wisdom's
sons and daughters."
Sophia/Wisdom has built a house.
S/HE has set a table, saying:
"Eat, drink, celebrate life,
and cherish Our creation."

✧ Eve and the Garden

The woman preferred the wild places along the banks of the river that flowed through the fertile crescent. She knew the forests. She loved the caves. She was one who ran with wolves, they said, for she talked to all that came to drink from the river's pristine waters.

One day she followed the river out and into a beautiful garden. There were trees and flowers of every kind and berries ripe for harvest, but she was drawn to a fruit-bearing tree in the middle of the garden. It was thick with buds and fragrant. *"As an apple tree among the trees of the wood, so is my Beloved,"* she sang, weaving in and out in a circle dance in the middle of the garden. Evening came, and she climbed the tree and fell asleep in its branches.

She went to the river at first light, and it was there that she saw him. *"Adamha,"* she whispered, "color of earth." She was glad that he was sleeping. As she drew near, the man awoke. "Here is one like me," he cried aloud, yet he saw that she was different. She had hair the color of wheat. She was full bodied and full breasted. He thought of Lilith, his sister Lilith, with raven's hair and the heart of an eagle, and once again he was lonely, for the garden could not contain the one who was with him from the beginning, and so she flew away.

"Where have you come from?" he asked the woman, and she pointed to the east. "I am caretaker of the garden," he said, and he turned in all directions, claiming as far as the eye could see. "Here it is paradise," he whispered. "Stay here in the garden with me."

Evening came and morning came to the woman and man in the garden. As he watched the woman from a distance, the man felt very good. She was full of life and spirit. She swam in the cool, clear water, sang with the birds, laughed at the antics of spiders and ants, danced among the growing things, and wore flowers in her hair. She played with all the animals, and she called them by their names. At dawn he could hear her chanting, but it was in the cool of the evening that he walked and talked with God.

Late one night, when the moon was full, he saw her dance with serpentine steps by the tree in the middle of the garden. *"Your love is better than wine,"* she sang, *"therefore we maidens love You, and we rejoice in You."* He was frightened by her rituals. The next day he said to her, "You must stay away from the fruit-bearing tree." "Why?" she asked, for she could see that he was deeply troubled. "Because God has commanded," he said. "But why?" she persisted. "Because it is a tree of death. Eat, and you will die." "It is a tree of life," she said, "a place of wisdom and knowledge, for Godde meets me there and helps me to know what is good and what is evil, so I can grow to be more like Godde." They spoke no more of her different ways, nor of the tree in the middle of the garden.

One day, when the tree was heavy with fruit, blood red and succulent, he saw the woman resting there, fair and desirable. *"You are beautiful, my love, so beautiful, a lily of the valleys,"* he sang, as he lay down beside her. She wakened to receive him. *"You are black and beautiful,"* she sang. *"My beloved is mine and I am his."* Evening came and morning came, witnessing to their love.

They were happy together as woman and man, transparent to each other, baring their deepest feelings, their fantasies and fears. To him she was life in all its fullness, and he called her by her name. She was Eve and he was Adam. She would laugh and say she too was of the earth and knew its blessings. Time passed, and Eve gave birth, by the tree of life in the garden. *"Sustain me with fruit, refresh me with apples, for I am faint with love,"* Adam sang, when the child could leave its mother. Eve gave birth a second time in the season of fruitfulness.

Eve and her daughters swam in the water, sang with the birds, danced among the growing things, and wore flowers in their hair, and once again, Adam was lonely. The womenfolk played by the apple tree, told stories and made ritual, and even talked to serpents and snakes. Surely, he thought, this foolish behavior cannot be pleasing to God. Adam talked with God in the evening, while Eve and her daughters chanted at dawn and when the moon was full. Adam knew his world was slipping away, for he could no longer control it. He began to hide himself from Eve, to cover his thoughts and feelings. He had lost his earthly paradise. One day, when he could bear it no longer, he let the woman lead him to a place beyond the garden, for Adam knew, as Eve knew, that Eden was no more.

✧ Eve's Sons, Cain and Abel _____

They settled east of Eden. Eve gave birth to a son, Cain, who was pleasing to his father. She bore a second son, and she named the baby Abel. "You are bone of my bone and flesh of my flesh," she whispered to her secondborn, the apple of her eye.

Cain grew to be a gardener, preferring to follow his father's ways, while Abel was a shepherd. Cain was jealous of Abel, who was his mother's favorite and who joined with her and their sisters to mark the feasts and festivals, the seasons and the harvests, and to make thank offerings in early spring when the ewes of the flocks were dropping their lambs, and when the cows were calving.

One day Cain called to his brother. "Let us go to the fields," he said, and the two went off together, downhill to a distant pasture. There Cain built an altar of stone. "We will sacrifice to God," he said, and he took one of the newborn lambs and laid it upon the altar. When Abel protested, Cain was enraged, and he attacked his brother, spilling his blood upon the ground and staining the stones crimson. Suddenly, Cain's heart was filled with fear. "I am cursed," he cried. "I will have to flee. I am forced to live like a fugitive. Where will I go, for I bear the mark of my brother's blood upon me?"

As Cain was coming up from the fields, he was met there by his mother. "Cain, where is your brother?" she asked. "How shall I know?" he said to her. "Am I my brother's keeper?" Pain pierced her through and through. "The blood of your brother cries out to me, the blood of my womb is calling to me," she said, weeping and wailing, and she could not be comforted. Adam would have avenged the sin, an eye for an eye, a life for a life, but Eve had had more than enough of death. "Shall I lose two sons to violence?" she cried, as she stayed the hand of her husband. And when the moon was high in the sky, she sent Cain away to her family, somewhere east of Eden. There, one day, he would take a wife who would bear him a son, Enoch. He would live to see his children's children. However, neither Eve nor Adam ever heard from him again.

✧ East and West of Eden

Eve gave Adam another son. She named him Seth, one sent by Godde to soothe her in her sorrow. Eve and Adam lived many years and had other sons and daughters. Although love and life and laughter prevailed within Eve and among her children, it was not so for Adam. The losses of Eden and Abel and Cain were more than he could bear. He talked of having tasted forbidden fruit and the price he had paid for his dalliance. Eve heard him singing to himself one night: *"Under the apple tree, I awakened. . . . There your mother was in labor with you; there she who bore you labored."* And she heard him saying to Seth one day: "In labor a woman reaps fruit of her womb; we labor to bring forth fruitful harvests. By the sweat of our brow must we make up for the lost legacy of Eden." Eve, however, accepted life, its cycles of abundance and absence, its rhythms of receiving and letting go, and she taught her daughters to honor their seasons in the sacredness of their bodies.

Before she died, Eve gave her youngest daughter a small clay figurine she had made long ago from the mud of the river in their father's fabled garden. She also gave her some shells from the sea, which she had brought with her into the garden. "Treasure these *teraphim*," she said, "and hand them on to your youngest daughter, and to her daughter's daughter." Then she and her sisters were given a branch, an *asherah,* from the fruit-laden tree beside their home, the site of their rites and rituals. "Let this be for you a tree of life," Eve said to each of her daughters, "for this tree is the offspring of the tree of life in the middle of the garden of Eden. It grew from a seed of the fruit of that tree, just as you have grown from a seed in my womb." Then Eve blessed each of her daughters, saying: "Cherish earth. Stay close to all living things, and your love will always be fruitful. Through trees and seas and moon and stars, through kinship with the animals, may your joys increase and multiply and fill the world with blessings. May Shekinah be with you and your children's children as Wisdom and Shalom."

Families, clans, and kinship circles increased and multiplied. To east and west, to north and south there was peace, and there was harmony, from generation to generation, as the daughters of Godde met and married the sons of women and men. Those were the days of the Amazons and other legendary women,

whose gifts of creativity and culture at the dawn of civiliza-
tion were the heart and soul of life. Naamah, daughter of Zillah,
could trace her lineage back to Cain, but she was her mother's
daughter. Known far and wide as a singer of songs, she led the
women in timbrel and dance as they spun their tales of moth-
ering and magic to continue their traditions. Zillah's husband,
Lamech, had a second wife, Adah, and she too had a daughter. Jubal, who played the lyre and pipe, was a marvelous music
maker. Her rippling melodies spilled down the hills and echoed
through the valleys as she and her sister, and all their sisters,
played and praised and worshiped.

As time passed, men grew restless. They competed for position, they craved prestige. Some who sought to be like gods
overpowered one another and changed their way of life. They
subdued their women and divided their children, labeling their
daughters inferior, and made all who opened the womb sub-
servient to the firstborn male. It was said around circles on
moonlit nights, where women would secretly gather to honor
their myths and their memories, that S/HE was weeping and,
one day soon, would deluge earth with tears.

✦ Noah and the Flood _____

Noa was a man of integrity in his generation. Noah, his wife,
was descended from those legendary women who had kept faith
with tradition. She and her daughters and the wives of her
sons celebrated the cycles of birth and rebirth together with all
of creation. She was known far and wide as a woman of wisdom, as one who discerned the presence of Godde, a healer
of body and spirit. Her husband loved and respected her. He
had been heard to say that he knew that she had found favor
with God.

One day the rains began to fall when it was not their season. For seven days and seven nights they continued unabated, as thunder and lightning and violent winds toppled tents and flooded fields and made the cattle fearful. Noah's husband cried to God, but Noah was strangely silent. She began to assemble flour and grain beside her *teraphim.*

The winds ceased but the rains continued once the storm had relented. The family's tents, pitched high on a hill, were deemed to be out of danger, even as flood waters swirled and rose in the valley far below them, yet Noah said to her husband: "We must build an ark, one large enough for all of us here, and the animals. Earth will be reborn in the waters flowing from the womb of Godde." Her words had the ring of an oracle. To hear was to obey.

Now the man was not a carpenter, nor could he imagine a seaworthy vessel big enough to accomplish the task. So he prayed to God as he gathered the wood, and then he and his sons constructed an ark according to a vision of cypress and pitch, many cubits in length, many cubits in width and height and depth, with cubicles and stalls, a roof, and doors to seal off the elements. As rain fell and the waters rose and wildlife moved up the mountain, hammering continued until water reached the threshold of Noah's hearth.

"Come, it is time to go," she said, moving among the animals, the sheep and goats of their domestic flocks, their oxen and their cattle. She herded them into the rough-hewn ark in what seemed to be family units, two at a time with their lambs and kids, and calves too small to be counted, as many as could be accommodated, including the untamed animals and frightened birds and insects. Two by two, with their little ones, all the wild animals seeking safety there at Noah's refuge went up into the ark, together with Noah's husband and sons, their wives and babies, Noah's daughters, and their precious *teraphim.* When all the food and drink had been stowed, Noah asked a blessing from Godde, and then she boarded the vessel. The ark floated off the hillside, leaving all they had loved behind. They could only hope that their friends in the valley had also sailed safely away.

It rained for forty days and forty nights. Everything was desolate. It seemed as though the waters extended the length and breadth of earth. The valleys and hills had all disappeared before the billowing deluge. No living thing outside the ark ever came into view. Noah's husband heard God's voice thundering across the water. Noah spoke of Godde's motherly love as dependable and deep. Then one day the rains ceased and the flood waters slowly subsided. A warm wind blew the clouds away. The sun absorbed some moisture. Even so, it would be a long, long time before dry land appeared. Eventually, Noah sent out a dove, but there was nowhere for it to settle, so it flew back to the ark. After seven days, for the second time, the dove flew toward the horizon and returned to them in the evening with an olive branch in its beak. Seven days later, the dove flew away. Their ordeal was finally over. As the waters receded, mountains appeared and, after a time, the valleys. Then all living creatures stepped out of the ark onto the newly washed land.

✧ Godde's Covenant with Noah _____

Noah's family pitched their tents, grateful for safe passage. They never returned to their former home. All who had journeyed on the ark, people and plants and animals, remained where the ark had come to rest and set out to begin again. Noah took her *teraphim* into a grove of flowering trees where she gathered with her family to give thanks and praise to Godde. "The womb waters of Shekinah precede rebirth and re-creation," she sang, as tales of deliverance were told and retold in their songs and in the dance.

In the pristine freshness of a whole new world, Noah knew

intimately S/HE Who Is. Godde entered into a covenant there with Noah and her descendants, with her children and their children from generation to generation, with the trees and the seas and the animals, with every living, breathing thing, and with stones and stars and planets. Godde entered into a covenant, saying: "Respect and honor all of life; hallow and protect one another. Never again do violence or harm nor allow evil to triumph. Have no dominion over others, but live as brothers and sisters with all that lives on earth." Suddenly, a rainbow appeared in the sky. Then Godde said to Noah: "This is the sign of the covenant we make, you and I and all that lives, for all future generations. See this and remember: there is an everlasting covenant between Godde and every living creature and among all that live on earth." Then Noah said to her daughters and sons,

"Neither last born nor first born, but let all the children inherit the blessings of earth."

✧ The Tower

Now men among the ruling classes spoke a similar language of power and control. They said, "Let us build a structure to assure our ascendancy." So they built a system, brick by brick, that towered over others. It even reached into the heavens, affecting the myths and heroes of old in the pantheons of their gods. But Godde saw their folly and laughed. S/HE planted a spark of intuitive resistance in the women of their households, so that sister and brother, wife and husband, peasant and patriarch, prophet and priest no longer understood one another. Confusion spread, and chaos ensued. Women who heard of men's foolishness said: "It sounds like empty babble." They called it the Tower of Babel, so that all who heard would remember and resist, even to this day.

TRADITIONS
OF THE MATRIARCHS
AND OTHER
MEMORABLE WOMEN

✧ Sarah the Matriarch ⸻

Sarah lived with her mother and brother on the banks of the river Balith, a tributary of the Euphrates in northern Mesopotamia, an area that came to be known as Haran, which was her brother's name. Her father lived with his second wife in Ur, which was in Sumer, also in Mesopotamia and on the Euphrates River, but much further south. Haran was married and had two daughters, whose names were Milcah and Iscah, and a son whose name was Lot. Their heritage was matrilineal. Sarah and her niece, Milcah, her brother's youngest daughter, would continue their kinship line. Now Terah, father of Sarah and Haran, was also the father of Abraham and Nahor, with whom he lived in Sumer.

One day Terah, with Abraham and Nahor, journeyed north to his other family, for his sons were now of an age to marry and were seeking suitable wives. They arrived in Haran and remained there. In the fullness of time, Terah died and was buried in Haran. Nahor married Milcah. He accepted her matristic culture and moved in with her family. Abraham, however, was restless, for his father's home was not his home. He longed to leave for places unknown. He might even go to Canaan. He spoke of this to his nephew Lot, who was eager to accompany him.

Now Abraham was attracted to Sarah, who was his father's daughter, but by another wife. He hoped that they could marry and that she would be willing to leave her kindred to make a life with him. Sarah withdrew to consider. She was descended from matriarchs, while Abraham lived in a different world, with strange views of lineage and an unfamiliar God. He said he loved to travel, while she was drawn to solitude and wanted her family near. He promised to make a home for her somewhere beyond her universe, saying God would provide the land. Sarah, deeply spiritual, turned to her *teraphim* to seek wisdom from S/HE Who Is. Abraham had said God was calling him out of Ur and out of Haran. Could this mean that he too was led by Godde, and that Godde wanted her to go with him? Sarah prayed for guidance. When Abraham asked her again, she consented, and she became his wife.

✧ Journey into Canaan _____

They journeyed south on the caravan route, Abraham and Sarah with their nephew Lot, and with all of their goods and possessions, his faithful servant, her personal maids, and her sacred *teraphim.* They entered the land of Canaan and continued on to Shechem, where they set up camp with the intention of remaining there for a while. They planned to travel in stages down to the Negeb further south.

At Shechem, Sarah took her *teraphim* to the sacred oak at Moreh and worshiped Asherah there, renewing Godde's covenant with Noah and promising to be faithful in this new and foreign land. Shechem was a religious center known for its commerce and trade. Abraham and Lot met with the merchants to exchange some personal property for sheep and goats, donkeys and camels, combining their separate livestock into several substantial herds.

After resting a while in Shechem, they continued south to the hill country, just to the east of Beth-el, where they pitched their tents and pastured their flocks. Abraham built an altar of stone and called upon El Shaddai. He inquired if they were to settle there, and if this were his promised land. Time passed, and there was famine throughout the land of Canaan. It grew so severe that Abraham decided they would seek some respite in Egypt. It was a long and difficult journey, through the Negeb and the wilderness of Shur. There were times when it seemed they might not make it, but Sarah trusted Shekinah, and Abraham, El Shaddai.

✦ Sarah with Pharaoh in Egypt ⎯⎯⎯⎯⎯⎯

Sarah and Abraham and Lot, with their servants and their live-stock, set up camp in Egypt at a place where others had also come seeking refuge from the famine. They had grain and oil, they could pasture their flocks, and they were able to form some bonds of friendship among the aliens there. Sarah met with the womenfolk who sought her out for counsel. Word of her wis-dom was whispered abroad and reached the ear of Pharaoh, who was seeking the advice of a seer. His household had been af-flicted with injuries and sickness, and his wives were not with child. He inquired after Sarah, and then he sent for her.

Sarah arrived at Pharaoh's palace accompanied by her hus-band, his servant, and her maid. Pharaoh, impressed by what he had heard, expected someone older and was taken by surprise, for Sarah was very beautiful. When Abraham saw how he looked at her, he feared for his own safety for Pharaoh's reputation was known far and wide. It was said that he had a harem filled with women of every culture, and that he had numerous wives. Abra-ham presented Sarah to Pharaoh and said, "She is my sister," so that if Pharaoh wanted Sarah, he would not lose his life. It seemed his fears were justified, for Pharaoh invited her into his chambers and sent Abraham away. Sarah insisted, however, that she be accompanied by her maid.

Now Sarah counseled Pharaoh and was able to console him. Her wisdom was reassuring, and he was taken with her beauty. When he asked for her in marriage, she replied, "I already have a husband." Pharaoh was extremely angry, and he would have disposed of Abraham if Sarah had not pleaded for his life. So he assured her of Abraham's safety and sent her away with some personal tokens of affection and esteem. When all that Sarah had said to him eventually came to pass, when there was peace again in his household and babies in the wombs of his wives, he sent generous gifts to her, donkeys and camels and oxen and sheep, and a large supply of food. He also sent an Egyptian girl, the daughter of his favorite concubine, who would be for Sarah a personal attendant. The young girl's name was Hagar.

✧ Return to Canaan

Sarah left Egypt with Abraham and Lot and all of their flocks and possessions, their male servants and female servants, and Hagar, Sarah's maid. They planned to return to Beth-el, a long journey to the north of Canaan, and would stop on the way at Beer-sheeba and Hebron in order to rest their flocks.

✧ Sarah and Abimelech

They came into the Negeb, but instead of continuing on the road, they turned toward Gerar, which lay to the west of Beer-sheeba, and stopped to sojourn there. Now Abimelech, the regional ruler, saw Sarah in the marketplace and marveled at her beauty. When he inquired as to who she was, he was told of how she had charmed Pharaoh and brought peace to his household, for some of his people had been in Egypt during the height of the famine and were witness to what had occurred. She had unusual powers, they said, and she was very wise. Abimelech sent for Sarah, that he might see these things for himself, and she arrived with Abraham. "She is my sister," Abraham said, presenting her to Abimelech, for once again he was wary, having been through this before.

Abimelech invited Sarah and Abraham into his inner courtyard, and he was so impressed with her that he decided to make her his wife. He inquired of Abraham the bridal price, but Sarah refused his advances, saying, "I am already married. Abraham is my husband." Abimelech was very angry. "Why have you done this thing?" he said. "Why say, 'She is my sister'?" "Because she is my sister," said Abraham, "the daughter of my father but not the daughter of my mother; and she is also my wife." It took some time before Sarah could convince Abimelech to release them. So that Sarah might think well of him and intercede with her Godde on his behalf, he gave her a thousand pieces of silver and a number of sheep and oxen. He also said to Abraham, "My land lies before you. Settle wherever you please." Then Sarah blessed Abimelech's household. "May the wombs of your wives be fruitful," she said, "and may all who are hurting be healed." They left Abimelech's presence, and she and Abraham and all who were with them journeyed on from there to Beer-sheeba.

✧ The Journey North ────────────────

They set up camp in Beer-sheeba, where they planned to remain to refresh their flocks and replenish their supplies. The journey from Egypt through the wilderness of Shur and the parched, dry land of the Negeb had been difficult for the animals. Abraham and Lot went into the village to negotiate with the merchants, acquiring more goats and sheep and camels, as well as flour and oil. Abraham also inquired about purchasing land, for this was Abimelech's territory and he had said they could settle there. Abraham was still uncertain about where El Shaddai was leading him. As he moved about in the public square and through the streets of the village, he chanced upon a beautiful woman, not once, but several times. He asked who this young woman might be, and if she had a husband. They said her name was Keturah, and she was still at the home of her father.

When the livestock and servants were rested and ready to move on, they departed from Beer-sheeba. As soon as they arrived in Hebron, Sarah went to the terebinth grove. She wished that Abraham would find his place and end their nomadic wandering. If only they could live in Hebron, she prayed, for Sarah knew deep down in her heart that this was her spiritual home. Before they broke camp to continue their journey, Sarah buried her precious *teraphim* in a shaded spot at the edge of the grove, near the oaks of Mamre.

✧ The Separation of Abraham and Lot ___

They came at last to Beth-el, where Abraham had built an altar and had felt the presence of God. They would pitch their tents and wait there until God gave them direction. Abraham had planned to live in Beth-el, which was why they had come there from Egypt, but now he was not so certain. They would have to wait and see.

Their camp spread out and into the valley, for the livestock of Abraham and Lot were many and required a lot of pasture. It was difficult keeping the herds apart. There was strife between Lot's men and those who worked for Abraham, with accusations of missing animals and concerns about such things as overgrazing and lack of water. It was clear to Abraham that he and Lot had to decide on separate routes. They had spoken of this several times before, but Lot had been reluctant. After all, Sarah and Abraham were family. Where else was he to go? This time Abraham insisted. They walked together to the top of a hill where the land below was an open plain that reached to the far horizon, pasture in every direction, as far as the eye could see. Abraham turned and said to Lot, "You and I are kindred. Let us be at peace. Your herds and mine have grown so large and our tents have become so many, there is no longer room enough for us to continue on together. Separate from me. The whole land lies before you. Choose where you would go. If you turn right, then I will go left. If you walk west, then I will go east. There is room enough here for both of us, but only if we live apart." Lot looked all around him, and he saw that the Jordan plain was like a watered garden, so he chose the river Jordan and the fertile grasslands there. He embraced Abraham and Sarah, asked each of them for a blessing, then headed east in the direction of Zoar and settled down in Sodom.

With the departure of Lot, Sarah lost a vital link to her lineage and culture. Now only Abraham shared her past, but who would share her future? She felt alone in an alien society, wed to a wandering Aramean who would pull up stakes again and again as he searched for his promised land. She prayed to Godde for patience and strength, and Godde said to Sarah, "Wherever you go, I will go." Sarah felt Shekinah within her, and she was comforted.

Abraham returned to his altar of stones, and there he cried out to El Shaddai. "O God, how shall I continue, for Sarah and I are childless. She has given me no heir." Then Abraham had a vision. He heard God's voice saying to him, "Look up at the heavens and count the stars, that is, if you are able to count them, for so shall your descendants be. Settle in the land of Canaan. Wherever you will be, I will be." Both Abraham and Sarah had received a word of comfort and consolation, and their hearts were at peace again.

Now Abraham knew that Sarah was grieving over the loss of

her kinsman Lot, and that she loved the oaks of Mamre, for it was there that she felt at home. So he said, "We will settle in Hebron," for he knew that wherever they pitched their tents, God would be with them there. Perhaps the oaks and the terebinth grove might do what he had been unable to do, bring him offspring from Sarah's womb. So they packed up all their possessions and journeyed down to Hebron, where Sarah purchased a parcel of land adjacent to the terebinth grove and established her tent in the shade of the oaks where she had buried her *teraphim*. Sarah was very happy there. For the rest of her life, she would never again depart from Kiriath-arba, which is the ancients' name for Hebron.

✧ Keturah

After some time, Abraham took leave of Sarah and departed for Beer-sheeba, for he had business to attend to. He went in search of Keturah, and he took her for his wife. Then he purchased land and dug a well, and established a household there.

Now Abimelech's servants were angry that Abraham had returned to Beer-sheeba to take up residence among them. They recalled how he had deceived their leader, so in retaliation they seized the well he had dug for Keturah. Abraham went to Abimelech to negotiate a peace. "I swear I will not deal falsely with you," Abraham said to Abimelech, "neither me nor my descendants. Let me settle on the land you promised me, so that I may no longer be an alien here, but may live among the people." Then he complained to Abimelech about the well his servants had stolen. Abimelech said to Abraham, "I do not know who has done this, for I have not heard of it until now, but it will be returned to you, and you may dwell here on the land." Then Abraham gave Abimelech seven ewe lambs as a witness that he himself had dug the well and had been given the rights to its waters. Abraham and Abimelech swore an oath and made a covenant in Beer-sheeba, saying that Abraham was no longer an alien there and was entitled to his plot of land.

Abraham returned to Keturah, and he stayed with her for many days. Keturah became pregnant, and bore a son, and Abraham named him Zimran. After eight days he circumcised the child, just as he himself had been circumcised, and he called upon El Olam, whose name means "Eternal God." He planted a tamarisk tree near the well before he left Beer-sheeba. Then he returned to Hebron and Sarah. Keturah remained behind.

✧ Sarah and Hagar ─────────────────

Now Sarah learned of Keturah, how she had given Abraham a son. Sarah understood that her husband, like their father before him, needed a second household where he could be patriarch, for the customs of the matriarchs were foreign to his ways. Although Abraham's need had been satisfied, Sarah was troubled, for she had no child to continue her kinship line. Then Sarah looked at Hagar and saw that she was beautiful, and that she had come of age, for she bled in the ways that women do and she had never known a man. It had been ten years since she had come to them, and she had served her mistress well. Hagar was more friend than servant; she was Sarah's steady companion, and she understood her ways.

One day Sarah called Hagar aside and told her what she had in mind, and asked if Hagar were willing. "I am," Hagar replied. She felt honored to be surrogate mother for Sarah so that she might continue her kinship line. The child of her womb would be Sarah's child, and Abraham would be the father. When Sarah told Abraham of their plan, he said that he too was willing. So

Sarah gave Hagar to Abraham as wife that she might give Sarah a child.

Abraham slept with Hagar until she knew she was pregnant. As the weeks passed, Sarah could see that something in Hagar had changed. She no longer confided in Sarah. She was reluctant to do her appointed tasks. Sarah went to Abraham. "What is it that you have said to her? Why is she treating me so?" "Hagar is your responsibility," he replied. "Why complain to me? Why not speak to her?" So Sarah drew Hagar aside to determine the cause of their conflict. "Now that I am pregnant," Hagar said, "and carrying the master's child, I want to be its mother. I want a household of my own, just like you and Keturah. Abraham said he would do this for me, but only if you were willing, and if he could circumcise my baby, should it be a boy." Sarah was angry. She felt betrayed. In the days that followed, she was hostile toward Hagar. She treated her like a servant, but Hagar felt more like a slave. The tension increased until Hagar could take no more of Sarah's silence, no more of her insensitivity. She decided to run away.

Hagar wrapped some food in a cloth, filled a skin with water, and went off into the wilderness, for nothing was going right for her and she did not know what to do. She could not go back to the way it had been, and she could not endure the way it was, so she sought refuge in the desert, away from the hurt in Sarah's eyes and the disappointment she was feeling. She fell asleep and an angel found her by a spring of water in the wilderness, between Hebron and Beer-sheeba. "Hagar, sister of Sarah, where have you come from and where are you going?" the angel called to her. "I am running away from my mistress," she replied. The angel said, "Return to her, for she means you no harm. She will do justice by you." Then the angel announced to Hagar: "You have conceived and shall bear a son, and you shall call him Ishmael. Your offspring will be too numerous to count, and I will multiply your blessings, for I have seen your affliction." Then Hagar rose up from her vision. "You are El Roi," she said, which means, "You are a God who sees," naming the one who had spoken to her. "I have seen the God who has seen me, and I am alive again."

Hagar arose and returned to Sarah, and she bore a son to Abraham, and named him Ishmael, which means "God hears." Abraham circumcised the boy and gave him back to Hagar. Sarah renounced her right to the child, returning Ishmael to his natural mother. She made a place for Hagar, a tent beyond the terebinth grove for the mother of Ishmael. Out of deference to her mistress, Hagar avoided Abraham and did not sleep with him again.

Abraham went down to Beer-sheeba and did not return for a very long time. Keturah gave Abraham other sons, Jokshan, Medan, and Midian. Hagar weaned Ishmael, content to watch the boy grow more like his father every day. Sarah retired to her tent in the grove, in seclusion with her *teraphim,* and remained close to Godde.

✧ Sarah's Motherhood _____

Abraham, who had returned to Hebron, was sitting by the entrance to his tent, in the full heat of the day. Sarah his wife was inside her tent preparing to offer worship. She had made cakes and was carefully arranging a cloth and her *teraphim,* when suddenly she heard, "Sarah." "Who is it?" she asked, for she saw no one. "Who calls me by my name?" "Sarah," said the voice, "you know who I am. I your Godde will bless you. You shall give rise to nations, and leaders shall come from you. You, Sarah, shall bear a son, and you shall name him Isaac. Our covenant is everlasting. I will return this time next year, and you will give birth to Isaac, and your joy will be complete." Suddenly, it was silent, and Sarah knew it had been the voice of S/HE who is her Godde. "His name will be Isaac," she said, and laughed. "My child,"

she said, and laughed and laughed, for Isaac means "laughter." Sarah's laughter rose from the depths of an indescribable joy.

Now Abraham, asleep in the heat of the day, also had a vision, which seemed like a waking dream. He looked up and saw three strangers there, a stone's throw from his tent. He hurried to meet them, bowing low to the ground, and said, "If it pleases you to favor me, do not pass me by. Let me bring you water to wash your feet; then rest yourselves a while. Sit under this tree, away from the sun, and I will bring you food and drink." They said, "Let it happen as you say." Abraham ran to Sarah. "Quickly," he said, "prepare some cakes." Then he took a tender calf from the herd and, when the meal was ready, brought curds and milk and the calf that was cooked and set it before his guests, who sat in the shade of a sheltering tree. He waited nearby until they were done. Then one of the visitors said to Abraham, "I will return to you in due season, and Sarah shall have a son." Then as suddenly as they had appeared to Abraham, just as quickly they were gone.

Abraham awoke to the sound of laughter coming from Sarah's tent. He went to her, and once again they knew they had both been visited by S/HE who is always with them. Now Sarah had been childless for all these many years. Whether it was because, as some have said, her religious and spiritual practices bound her to foreswear motherhood, and so she had never been with Abraham as a man is with his wife, or had been with him at times and in ways that prevented her pregnancy, indeed, whether the cause was physical or spiritual, no one will ever know. What was known is that Sarah was childless, and that other women, Hagar and Keturah, were the mothers of Abraham's sons. Yet on this day Abraham approached Sarah in the sanctity of her tent, and Sarah became pregnant, and both Sarah and Abraham laughed.

Godde was gracious to Sarah. She gave birth to a beautiful baby in the season of her fulfillment, just as S/HE had promised, and she named her son Isaac, saying: "God has given laughter to me, and all who hear will laugh with me, saying: 'Who would

ever have said to Abraham that Sarah would nurse his child?' "
All of her household rejoiced with her, Abraham and Hagar and
Ishmael, maid servants and men servants, while local midwives
marveled. On the eighth day, there was a feast, but Abraham did
not circumcise the boy, for Isaac was Sarah's child.

Now Sarah sent word to Milcah, and Milcah's sister Iscah, in-
quiring about their families, and if they had borne a daughter
who one day might marry her son. Isaac was chasing butterflies
by the time the news got back to her. Iscah had died in childbirth, and she had left no heirs. Milcah had given Nahor seven
sons: Uz and Buz and Kemuel, Chesed, Hazo, Phildash, and their
youngest boy, Jidlaph. She had also given birth to Bethuel, who
was her only daughter, and she had a daughter, Rebekah. Nahor
had taken a second wife, like his father and his brother Abraham, a local girl named Reumah, who was mother to Tebah,
Gaham, and Tabash, and a daughter named Maacah. Reumah's
daughter, however, was not a suitable heir, for Maacah's mother
Reumah was outside their kinship group. From that moment
on, Sarah began preparing for a marriage between Isaac and
Bethuel's child.

✧ The Freeing of Hagar

When the child Isaac no longer needed his mother's breast for
sustenance, his father Abraham threw a feast to mark the day
of his weaning. The festivity was also a celebration of Ishmael's
coming of age. Sarah saw the son of Hagar playing with her
son Isaac, saw that the older boy was curious because Isaac was
uncircumcised. Suddenly her heart was filled with dread. Although Isaac was her matrilineal heir, here in this household of
Abraham's sons, Ishmael the firstborn, Ishmael the circumcised,
Ishmael the son of a patriarch was Abraham's legitimate heir.

Surely Abraham would arrange for Ishmael to marry within their family circle, and Sarah knew that their kinswoman, Rebekah, was the only available wife. Rebekah was promised to Isaac, but Isaac was still a little boy, while Ishmael was swiftly maturing. Who could say whether Abraham would agree to save Rebekah for Isaac when it came time for Ishmael to marry. "Ishmael will not marry Rebekah!" Of this, Sarah was certain, for that meant that her lineage would end with her. So Sarah made a decision concerning Hagar and Ishmael. "Promise me," she said to Hagar, "that you will find a wife for Ishmael from among your own people, and I will set you free." Hagar made that promise, and Sarah set her free.

On hearing this, Abraham was deeply distressed, for he loved the boy and his mother, who had lived so long with them. But he knew that in this household, he would do what Sarah told him, and Sarah had told Abraham that Hagar would be leaving, and that Ishmael would leave with her.

One morning, just before sunrise, Abraham filled a skin with water, wrapped some bread in a piece of cloth, and put these on Hagar's shoulder. He took sheep and goats from his choicest flock, and gave a shepherd's staff to Ishmael. He bound Hagar's possessions, together with food and tents and gifts, to a caravan of donkeys. Then they took leave of Hebron, Abraham and Hagar and Ishmael, and journeyed south to Beer-sheeba, where Abraham established Hagar's tent a short distance from Keturah's and told her to remain with him.

Neither Hagar nor Ishmael was happy there. They felt as though in a desert where the waters of life had all dried up. The boy cried out, and Hagar wept. Then a voice from heaven called to her. "Hagar, what is it that troubles you? Do not be afraid. I have heard the cry of your flesh and blood. Take the boy and care for him, for I will make of him a great nation." Then Hagar saw a well of water, and she and her son drank deep. With that, the vision vanished. Strength returned to Hagar. She said, "I will not see to the death of my child." She would leave Beer-sheeba and look for the oasis she had just envisioned, for her son was growing distant from her, and the pain of this felt to her as though an arrow had pierced her heart.

Abraham gave Hagar permission to go, and said he would travel with her to ensure her safe passage. They headed south through the Negeb, to the wilderness of Shur, then Abraham departed and returned to his home. Hagar established her house in the desert, by a source of running water. She made a home for Ishmael near the oasis of Paran, and God was with the boy. He became an expert with the bow and thrived in the wilderness. When it was time, Hagar secured a wife for him from Egypt.

Abraham returned to Beer-sheeba. Keturah gave him two more sons, Ishbak and Shuah. Many years passed before Abraham would return to Hebron again.

✧ Sarah's Sacrifice

Drawn by a need to see his son, Isaac, and to be once again with Sarah, Abraham returned to Hebron. There was rejoicing all around.

The moon had not yet run its course when Abraham arose and woke his son. "Come," he said. "Where?" asked Isaac. "We are going into the mountains." He saddled a donkey with food and drink, taking care not to awaken Sarah. They had reached the lower foothills by the time the sun was up. When Sarah arose, she was greeted by a silence in the compound. It would be three days before she would see her husband and son again.

They had gone a day's journey when Isaac asked, "What will we do in the mountains?" "We will worship God," said Abraham, "and we will offer sacrifice." At nightfall, they set up camp and then traveled well into the second day before reaching their destination. Abraham cut wood for an offering and gave it to Isaac to carry, while he brought the fire and the knife. The two walked on together until they came to a large overhang of rock the size and shape of an altar. "This is the place," said Abraham. "But where is the offering?" Isaac asked. "God will provide," replied Abraham.

After Abraham had made a small wood fire, he asked his son to take off his robe and lie down upon the altar. Puzzled, Isaac obeyed. Abraham held the knife in the fire, and then said a prayer to El Olam as he circumcised his son. Then Abraham said to Isaac: "God will indeed bless you, my son, with offspring as numerous as the stars in the sky and the sands beside the sea. Through your offspring shall all the nations of earth gain blessings for themselves." Then he threw the bloody cloth in the fire as a burnt offering to God.

Sarah saw from a distance that the two were returning home. When she observed how her son Isaac walked, she knew what Abraham had done to him and was overcome with grief. "How could you do this thing?" she cried, as Abraham was approaching. "God said to me, 'Keep my covenant, you and your offspring, through all generations. Circumcise the flesh of your foreskins, you and every male among you, for this is the sign of the covenant which I am establishing with you." Those were Abraham's words to Sarah. He said, "God also said to me: 'I will establish my covenant with Isaac, whom Sarah shall bear to you.'" Then Abraham retired to his tent and closed his heart to Sarah's grieving.

Sarah wept both night and day, for she was deeply troubled. One she loved had betrayed her trust. Now when she died, her lineage died, and her people would be no more. Days passed before reason returned. "For the sake of my son, for the sake of myself, I must reconcile two traditions," she said, "for there are both matriarchs and patriarchs in Isaac's ancestry. Why must circumcision separate blood from blood and bone from bone? El and Asherah, are they not one? El Shaddai, 'God of the Mountain,' and Shaddai, 'Godde the Breasted One,' are they not S/HE who is, now and always, everlasting love? Is not Shekinah the presence of Life in a multitude of guises?" So Sarah resolved to accept the conditions that Abraham had imposed on her. Isaac, the son of both Sarah and Abraham, would be heir to both of them. Isaac would inherit the covenant that Abraham had heard God promise, but he would also carry the tradition of his mother's matrilineal ways.

Sarah told Abraham what she had decided, and she made him promise to see to it that Isaac married Rebekah. "Swear," she said, "by the blood of our son, the blood that was spilled upon your hand, that the child formed from the blood of my womb will wed Rebekah when it is time." So Abraham swore an oath that day, there by the oaks of Mamre, and promised never to betray Sarah again, as long as they both should live.

✦ Sarah's Death and Burial _____

Although the two had reconciled, Abraham was ill at ease around Sarah. One day he went down to Beer-sheeba to stay. He never saw Sarah again. Abraham was in Beer-sheeba when word came to him. In the fullness of years, Sarah his wife, Sarah his sister had died.

Abraham went up to Hebron to weep and mourn for Sarah and to purchase a burial place for her. He said to the local leaders, "I am an alien among you. Give me property for a burying place, that I might bury my dead." "Choose what you will," they said to him. "We will not withhold from you even the best of places," for they knew Sarah and honored her as a woman of uncommon wisdom and great integrity. "Give me the cave of Machpelah," said Abraham, "with the field and all that is on it, as a burying place for Sarah." Then he paid four hundred shekels of silver to the owner of that land in the hearing of all the people. So the field in Machpelah to the east of Mamre, the field with the cave that was on it, and all the trees that were in the field, both oaks and terebinth, with the grove that Sarah held sacred, passed into the hands of Abraham as a burial place for Sarah and for those who came after her. Then Abraham buried Sarah his wife in the cave of the field of Machpelah, facing the oaks of Mamre, in the place called Kiriath-arba, which we now know as Hebron. Tradition has it that Sarah's death was a loss for all the people. Some say that as long as she was alive, all went well, but when she died, confusion enveloped the land.

✧ The Fate of Sodom and Gomorrah ____

Abraham was sitting at the entrance to his tent, out of the reach of the midday sun, when God came to visit. "Abraham," said God, "how great the outcry against Sodom and Gomorrah, and how heinous is their sin." "Will you destroy these cities?" asked Abraham. "And will you wipe out the innocent together with the wicked? What if you should happen to find fifty righteous people? Will you sweep them away as well? Shall not the Just One do what is just?" God said, "If I find in Sodom fifty righteous people, I will forgive all for their sake." Abraham said, "Pardon me for saying, for I am but dust and ashes, but suppose five are lacking. Will you destroy an entire city simply for the lack of five?" God said, "I will not destroy the city if I find forty-five people." Again Abraham interceded. "Suppose forty are found there?" God answered, "For the sake of forty, the city will be spared." Abraham said, "Forgive me if I persist, but suppose there are thirty there?" God answered, "I will not do it if I find thirty there." "Suppose there are twenty?" said Abraham. "For the sake of twenty people," said God, "the city will not be destroyed." Then Abraham pleaded, "Do not be angry if I speak once more, but suppose ten people should be found there?" God said, "For the sake of ten people, the city will be spared."

Then God finished speaking, and Abraham awoke to the memory of a dream he had had a long time ago. Three visitors, who had been guests at his table, had spoken of going to Sodom to seek after justice. Abraham was troubled, for his nephew Lot lived in Sodom. What on earth was happening there?

✧ Lot's Wife and Daughters

Now Lot had settled in Sodom after leaving Sarah and Abraham. He married a local woman and they had two beautiful daughters. Both would soon be married to men who were living in the town.

One evening two strangers came to Sodom while Lot was sitting at the city gate. As soon as he saw them, he greeted them and bowed low to the ground. "Please," he said, "come home with me and join me at my table. You can wash your feet, and spend the night, and be on your way again." "We will stay here in the square," they said. Lot persisted, until at last they agreed to go home with him.

Lot and his wife prepared a feast. He washed their feet and she baked bread, and they sat and ate their fill. Before the guests went off to rest, a mob of men surrounded the house and shouted insults to Lot, saying, "Where are the men who are with you tonight? Hand them over to us, so that we might have our way with them." Lot stepped out to reason with them and shut the door behind him. "I beg of you, my brothers," he said, "do not do such an evil thing. Look, I have two virgin daughters. Allow me to bring them out to you and you can do to them as you please, only do not violate these men who sought hospitality with me." But the mob responded, "Out of our way!" as they pushed Lot back against the door. "Who are you to judge us?" they asked. "You are a foreigner here. We will do even worse to you than we plan to do to your guests." They rushed to the door to break it down, but the guests reached out and pulled Lot in and barred the door behind him. Those who were pressing forward were suddenly struck by a blinding light. When they realized Lot and his guests were gone, they went elsewhere into the night.

The house guests said with some urgency, "Who else is there in your family? Have you relatives in Sodom? You must get them out of here. The city is about to be destroyed, because the outcry against the wicked has reached the ear of God." So Lot went after the two young men who were about to marry his daughters and said, "Get up, we must get out of this place, for God is about to destroy it." They thought that he was joking, so he left the men behind. When morning came, the visitors urged, "Take your wife and daughters and leave, or you will be completely destroyed in the punishment of this city." But Lot lingered, so the visitors seized him, his wife, and his two young daughters and led them forcefully by the hand out of the doomed city, because God would be merciful to them. The strangers were angels of God.

On the outer edge of the city, the angels said to Lot and his wife, "Run for your life. Do not look back or stop along the way. Cross the plain and head for the hills, or you will be consumed." Then Lot pleaded with the angels, "Oh, no, my friends, though you save my life with overwhelming kindness, I am afraid to flee to the hills where disaster might overtake me, and then I will surely die. Look, see that small town over there? It is near enough to run to. Spare that town, it is such a little place, and I will go there to escape God's wrath, and my family and I will be safe." "Very well," said the angels, "let it be so. We will not destroy that town, for it will be your place of refuge. Hurry, then, to the town of Zoar. You will find safety there."

Now Lot's wife had been listening to her husband's whining and pleading. He is thinking only of himself, she reflected. She looked at her lovely daughters and wept. If it had been up to their father, they would have been raped and brutalized by a mob the night before. Why should I run to the hills with him or even to the town of Zoar, she reasoned, and she looked back on the city, where all of her childhood memories mingled with her family's hopes and dreams. Then she kissed her daughters, turned around, and walked back into Sodom. The sun rose red and orange, as Sodom and Gomorrah went up in flames. All those inhabitants trapped in their homes — they say they were the wicked ones — perished in the fire. The smell of sulfur lingered, long after the smoke was gone. The tears of the women, it has been said, turned sweet well water brackish, and where the body of Lot's wife had fallen was found a pillar of salt.

Now Lot and his daughters arrived in Zoar, but he was afraid to remain there. The inhabitants eyed him suspiciously, for he had come from Sodom, which had been thoroughly corrupt. So Lot and his daughters went out from Zoar to live in a cave high up in the hills, for Lot had lost all his possessions and he had nowhere else to go. His daughters longed for the city but said: "Our father is old; we will care for him, for he has no one else to turn to."

One evening, when Lot was drunk with wine, he approached his elder daughter, and that night he slept with her. He was so intoxicated, he could not say when he lay down beside her or when she got up and left. The next day the firstborn said to her sister, "Last night I slept with my father," and the girl broke down and wept. She warned her younger sister, and they both avoided Lot. Then one night, drunk with wine, Lot uncovered his youngest child, and he was so intoxicated, he never knew that he lay with her or that she got up and left. The daughters were devastated. "We have been violated by our father. There is not a man remaining on earth who will come and marry us now." Soon after they saw that they were pregnant and, in due time, delivered sons. The firstborn named her baby Moab. Her sister named her boy Ben-ammi. Generations later the elder daughter would have a legendary descendant, a Moabite named Ruth.

✧ Rebekah

Now Abraham was well advanced in years when he said to his trusted servant, "I swore to Sarah that when it was time I would choose a wife for Isaac from among her kinship circle. Rebekah, Bethuel's daughter, the granddaughter of Milcah, my brother's wife, is waiting to marry Isaac. You must go to Rebekah and say to her, 'Isaac is waiting for you.' " The servant replied to Abraham, "What if the woman is unwilling to come back with me to Canaan? Shall I then take Isaac back again to the land from which you came?" "No," said Abraham, "he must not go back. God led me out of my father's house, led me away from the land of my birth, promising that my offspring would find blessings in this land. An angel will go before you. Rebekah will be waiting there. But if she is unwilling to return with you and chooses to remain in her mother's house, then you and I will be free from our oath. Now go, bring Rebekah here."

The servant took camels laden with gifts and maid servants to accompany the girl and left for the region of Aram-naharaim and the city of Nahor. At the outer edge of the city, at the time when women go forth to draw water, he settled his camels near the village well and prayed for a fruitful encounter. Scarcely had he finished praying when Rebekah, daughter of Bethuel, granddaughter of Milcah, approached the well with her water jar. She was lovely to look at, there at the spring, as she filled her jar with water. Now Abraham's servant had prayed for a sign. "The girl to whom I say, 'Please give me your jar that I may drink,' and who answers, 'Drink, and I will also water your camels,' let her be the one who has been chosen as wife for your servant Isaac." As the woman was coming up from the spring, the servant ran to meet her and said, "Please, give me a sip from your water jar," hoping the girl was Rebekah. "Drink, sir," the woman responded, and she graciously lowered her jar so that he could drink. When he had finished, she said to him, "I will draw water for your camels also, until they have had their fill." She emptied her jar into the trough and drew some more, and then some more, watering all his camels. The servant gave her two gold bracelets and a nose ring of finest gold. "Tell me whose daughter you are," he said. "Is there room in your father's house for all of us here to spend the night?" "I am the daughter of Bethuel, and the granddaughter of Milcah," she said. "We have food for you and the animals, and you are welcome to spend the night." "Blessed be the God of Abraham," he cried, bowing low to the ground. "God who has shown a steadfast love and has been faithful to my master has led me directly here to you and to my master's relatives." The girl ran ahead to tell her mother and all in her mother's household about what had just occurred.

When Laban, Rebekah's brother, heard his sister's excited words and saw the ring and the bracelets, he hurried out to the spring of water. "Welcome, O blessed servant of God," he said to Abraham's servant. "Why are you standing here outside? Our house is prepared to receive you." So Laban led them into the house, both male and female servants, and gave them water to wash their feet. Then he went to unload the camels, making sure that the animals had enough to eat. The womenfolk gathered around the fire, and Abraham's maids told many stories of how it had been with Sarah, and what it was like in that faraway land, and how they had heard about Rebekah ever since Sarah's Isaac was born.

When food had been set before Abraham's servant, he refused to eat until he had told them the reason why he had come. He recounted to Rebekah's family every detail of his journey, the oath, the sign, Rebekah's response, and inquired of Bethuel and Laban what it was they were prepared to do. "This, which has been arranged for years, has been confirmed by God," they replied. "There is nothing we can add. Rebekah has been promised to your master's son, as God has clearly shown us." With that, the servant took out several garments, and jewelry of silver and gold, and gave these to Rebekah. He also gave to her mother and brother some costly ornaments. Then he, and those who had accompanied him, ate, drank, and retired for the night.

They arose early the next morning. Abraham's servant was anxious. "I will return at once to my master," he said. "Rebekah must go with me." Her mother and brother pleaded with him. "Let the girl stay a little longer," they said. "After ten days, she may go." But the servant said, "I must not delay. My master is waiting to hear that God has made my journey successful. What if he dies before we return, for he is advanced in years and we have a very long way to travel." He also feared that if they tarried the girl might not go with him. Rebekah's mother and brother replied, "We will have to ask Rebekah. She is the one to decide." When they asked her, "Will you go with this man?" she responded, "Yes, I will." So Rebekah, along with her personal maid, prepared to leave for Canaan. Bethuel blessed her daughter, saying, "Daughter of ours, sister of ours, may you increase to thousands and tens of thousands! May all of your children's children live in wisdom and shalom." Then Rebekah and her maids mounted the camels and followed Abraham's servant, out of the embrace of Aram-naharaim, away from the warmth of her mother's home and the strength of the matriarch's circle, into the land of Canaan, where a whole new world was waiting. All along the journey, Rebekah clung to the *teraphim* that her mother Bethuel had given to her, which her grandmother Milcah had given her, which would pass from Rebekah to a child of her own and on to her children's children.

Now Isaac had returned from Beer-lahai-roi to his father's place in the Negeb. It was evening. He was walking out in the fields, just as the sun was setting, when he saw camels approaching from afar, mere shadows in the distance. Rebekah, seeing him walking there, asked: "Tell me, who is that man out there who is crossing the field to meet us?" Abraham's faithful servant said, "It is my master, Isaac." Hearing this, Rebekah slid from her camel and covered her face with her veil. Isaac came to greet them and brought them to his father. Together they listened to all that had happened and to stories of their ancestral home. Then Isaac took Rebekah and went up to Kiriath-arba, to the place that belonged to his mother. He led Rebekah into his mother's tent, and he took her for his wife. Isaac loved Rebekah, and his love for her was a comfort to him, now that his mother had died.

✧ Abraham's Legacy

Abraham had given Ishmael some of his prized possessions, including lambs and kids from his flocks. The children of Keturah he had supported while he had lived with them, and all six sons were established now with property and wives. When Abraham thought of Sarah his wife, he wished he had had a daughter, and he held a special place in his heart for Isaac, Sarah's son. He gave gifts to the sons of Hagar and Keturah, but he gave all that he had to Isaac, the whole of his inheritance, both property and the legacy of the promise made by God. At a good old age, Abraham died and was gathered to his people. Isaac and Ishmael buried him in the cave at Machpelah, in the field east of Mamre, beside his beloved Sarah, his sister and his wife. Then Isaac left Kiriath-arba at the urging of Ishmael and journeyed south with all his possessions to live in Beer-lahai-roi. He did not stay there very long.

✧ Rebekah's Twins, Esau and Jacob

Life was hard for Rebekah, for she felt like a stranger in an alien land, and she longed for her mother's home. For years, Rebekah was childless, yet Isaac loved her dearly. Although she could not give him sons, he never turned to a concubine, nor did he take a second wife, at least not that we know.

It was said that Rebekah was barren, but after much prayer and many tears, she discovered she was pregnant. At first, nothing on earth could match her excitement and her joy. As it grew closer to her time, her pains were fierce and frightening. She cried to Godde in desperation, and this was Godde's response. "Two forces are struggling within your womb, two peoples about to be born of you, who will grow to be divided. The stronger one will dominate, and the elder will serve the younger." Rebekah had heard her grandmother speak of the struggles endured by Sarah, the dominating ways of the patriarch, the pain of a divided heart. "If this is to be for me as well, then why should I go on living?" she cried from the depths of her despair.

When the time came for Rebekah to give birth, indeed there were twins in her womb. Her firstborn was red and hairy all over, so she named the baby Esau. The second was born clutching Esau's heel, and so she named him Jacob. Esau took after his father, while Jacob was his mother's son. Esau grew into a skillful hunter, and he remained a man of the fields. Isaac preferred Esau. Jacob, a quiet, more gentle man, spent most of his time around the tents. Rebekah loved Jacob.

Once when Jacob was busy preparing a tasty lentil stew, Esau came in from the field and said: "Let me have some of that food you are cooking." Jacob quickly replied, "I will, if you sell me your birthright." "What earthly use is a birthright to me when I am dying of hunger!" Esau replied, for he had been up since sunrise with nothing to eat all day. "Swear to me first," said Jacob. So Esau swore, and then and there, he sold his birthright to Jacob. Then Jacob gave Esau bread and stew. He ate and drank, and then got up and went away, unconcerned about his birthright.

Esau was the first to marry. He wed a Canaanite woman, which nearly broke his mother's heart. She had always expected her sons to take wives from within her kinship circle, the way it had always been done.

✧ The Blessing _____

When Isaac was old and nearly blind, he summoned his first-born, Esau, and said, "The day of my death is approaching. Take your weapon, go into the fields, and hunt some game for me. Prepare a dish of savory food. Let me eat and enjoy it one more time, before I return to my people. Then I will bless you before I die."

Now Rebekah overheard what Isaac had said, so she went to Jacob and conspired with him. "Your father sent Esau to hunt for game and to prepare a savory stew. He said that after he eats it, he will give Esau his blessing, for he is preparing to die. Quickly, take two choice kids from the flock and bring them here to me. I will prepare a savory dish, the kind your father enjoys, so that he will give his blessing to you and not to your brother Esau." "My brother Esau is a hairy man," Jacob said to his mother. "See my skin, how smooth it is. What if my father should feel me and discover our deceit? He may curse me, rather than bless me." "Let the curse be on me," Rebekah replied. "Just do as I have said."

So Jacob selected two choice kids, and his mother prepared a savory dish. It was Isaac's favorite. Then Rebekah wrapped Jacob in Esau's robes, and covered his skin with the skins of the kids, making his neck and hands hairy. She gave him the stew and the bread she had baked, and he took these to his father. As Jacob approached Isaac, he asked, "Who are you, my son?" "I am your firstborn, Esau," said Jacob. "I have done as you have requested. Enjoy this food, and bless me." But Isaac said to Jacob, "How did you find the game so quickly?" "God made me successful," he replied. Then Isaac said, "Come here to me and let me feel you, to be sure that you are Esau." So Jacob drew near to Isaac, who felt his hairy hands and said, "The voice is the voice of Jacob, but the hands are the hands of Esau." Still doubting, and unable to see, he asked, "Are you really Esau?" "I am," Jacob responded. "Then bring me the food, that I might eat, and afterward give my blessing." So Jacob gave him food and wine, and when he was finished eating and drinking, Isaac said to Jacob, "Come here and give me a kiss, my son." So Jacob kissed his father, who smelled the smell of his garments and blessed him with these words: "The smell of my son is the smell of a field that God has graciously tended and generously blessed. May God give you the dew of heaven, and the fatness of earth, and grain and wine in abundance. May you rise above your brothers. Cursed be the one who curses you, and blessed be those who bless you!"

When Isaac had finished blessing Jacob, and Jacob had departed, his brother Esau came in from the hunt with savory food for his father. "Come, eat this game, then bless me," he said. "Who are you?" asked Isaac. "I am your firstborn, Esau," he replied. Isaac was horrified and asked, "Then who was here before you? I ate his game and I blessed him. And the blessing cannot be recalled!" Esau screamed when he heard these words. "Bless me also, father," he cried. But Isaac replied with deep distress, "Your brother came in here deceitfully, and he has taken away your blessing." "Jacob!" shouted Esau. "How well he is named! For once again, he has supplanted me. He took away my birthright, and now he has stolen my blessing!" Then Esau pleaded with Isaac, "Have you no blessing for me?" Isaac said to Esau, "I have already put him in charge of you. I have made his brothers his servants. With grain and wine I have fortified him. What then can I do for you?" Esau wept. In despair he cried: "Have you only one blessing, father? Please, bless me too!" Then Isaac lifted his voice and said, "Your home shall be far from the fatness of earth and away from the dew of heaven. You shall serve your brother, but when you break free, you shall remove his yoke from your neck."

Now Esau hated Jacob, because he had stolen his blessing, and he plotted his revenge. "After we bury my father, I will kill my brother Jacob," he said. His wives went to Rebekah and told her of Esau's plans. She sent for Jacob and said to him, "Esau is planning to kill you. Flee at once to my family in Haran and stay with my brother Laban. When Esau's anger eases, and he forgets what you have done to him, you can return to Canaan. Wait until I send for you." As Jacob was about to slip away, Rebekah gave him her *teraphim* for guidance and protection. She may have sensed that she and her son would never meet again, that she was not to be the one to pass the matriarchs' traditions on to his daughters and their daughters. Rebekah instructed Jacob: "My brother Laban has two daughters. Take one of them as your wife. On the day you marry, give your bride these *teraphim* and say, 'May Shaddai bless you and make you fruitful. May the blessings of Sarah descend through you from generation to generation.'" Then Jacob left for Paddan-aram and the home of his mother's family, near the city of Haran.

✧ Judith, Basemath, Mahalath, Adah, Oholibamah _____

Esau had married Judith and taken her into his home. Then he married Basemath. Although the women were Canaanites and outside her matrilineal line, Rebekah quickly adjusted. She enjoyed having the women around. They were like daughters to her, and she grew quite fond of them. They shared in all that women do. They told stories, and now and then Rebekah would join in the dancing. They marked the seasons together with the rites of Asherah, and although they did things differently, what mattered was the same. Life was bitter for Isaac, however. He resented sharing his son with wives and disliked their different ways. Tensions eased when they began giving birth to Esau's sons.

With Jacob gone, Esau was determined to regain his father's favor. He knew that the Canaanite women he had married were not pleasing to Isaac, so he went to visit Ishmael, who was his father's brother. There Esau married Mahalath, the sister of Nebaioth. She was Ishmael's daughter. Esau went home and became the father of a number of sons and daughters.

One day Esau took his wives and children and the members of his household, his livestock and all that he had acquired while living in the land of Canaan, and moved some distance away. He was not happy in his father's home knowing it would soon be Jacob's home, for he was no longer heir. Esau was far from destitute. His flocks were so large that his father's land could not support both herds. So he left for the hill country of Seir and acquired property there. He would marry again, and yet again, but only after Isaac died. He took Adah, a local woman. Then he married Oholibamah. The records suggest he had only three wives, two Canaanites and Ishmael's daughter, that Judith and Adah were really the same, as were Basemath and Mahalath. Only the women know for sure. The writings say he had many sons and imply that he also had daughters.

✧ Jacob's Dream ————————————————————

It would be many years before Jacob would return to Canaan, the land of his birth. He would never see his father, Isaac, or his mother, Rebekah, again. He would not be the one who would bury them beside Sarah and Abraham in Hebron in the cave at Machpelah. All this, however, was unknown to him as he left his mother's presence. The last he ever saw of her was a shadow on the horizon, her long hair blowing in the wind, waving farewell to him. How clever and courageous she was, he recalled. He would return to that memory again and again, how she, a matriarch in a patriarch's home, had outwitted her husband to secure a blessing for the youngest of her sons.

The journey to Paddan-aram was long. It was best to do it in stages. Jacob left Beer-sheeba and continued traveling toward Haran, until he came to Beth-el. He decided to stay there for the night, for the sun was already setting. He took a stone, placed it under his head, and slept out under the stars. He dreamed he saw a ladder there, resting solidly on earth and reaching into heaven. Angels were ascending and descending, moving between heaven and earth. He dreamed S/HE was there beside him, saying, "I am the God of your fathers, of Abraham and of Isaac. I am the Godde of your mothers, of Sarah and Rebekah. The land on which you lie is holy. Know that I am with you and will keep you wherever you go. I will bring you back again to this place, where you and your heirs will be blessed."

Jacob awoke from his sleep and said, "Surely Godde is present, and I did not know it! Sacred is this place! I have stood at the gate of heaven, beheld the house of Shaddai." Jacob took the stone from beneath his head and set it up as a pillar. Pouring oil upon it, he said: "May God be with me and keep me in the way that I must go. May Godde sustain me with bread to eat and clothing to wear, until I come again to my mother's tent and can enter into my father's house with gladness and in peace."

✧ Rachel and Leah ─────────────────

Jacob arrived at the end of his journey and stopped by the one known water source for several towns and villages. Three flocks of sheep with their shepherds were waiting beside the well. "Where are you from?" Jacob asked. "From Haran," the shepherds responded. "Do you know Laban, son of Nahor?" he asked. "We do," said one of the shepherds. "Is it well with him?" "Yes," they replied. Some moments later, they said to Jacob, "Here comes his daughter Rachel." She was approaching with their sheep. Then Jacob said, "It is much too early to be gathering the sheep from their pastures. Why are you watering your flocks now?" The shepherds explained to Jacob, "We must wait until all the flocks are gathered before we uncover the well. We open the well only once each day and water all our sheep." Jacob saw that the stone covering the well was large and very heavy and that Rachel had arrived at the well.

While the shepherds were greeting Laban's daughter, Jacob removed the stone from the well and watered Rachel's sheep. Then he began to weep. She was startled when he kissed her. He said he was the son of her father's sister, her relative from afar. Rachel ran and told her father she had seen Rebekah's son. Laban ran to Jacob. He embraced him, and kissed him, and brought him to his house, rejoicing that he had lived to see his sister Rebekah's child. When Jacob had told him all the news and had praised his mother Rebekah saying that all was well with her, Laban said: "You are my flesh and bone," and he welcomed him into his home.

When Jacob had been there about a month, Laban approached him and said to him, "Even though you are my kinsman, this does not mean you should serve without pay. What shall I give you for wages?" Now Laban had two daughters. Leah was the older of the two; the younger one was Rachel.

Leah had lovely, dancing eyes that were always watching Jacob, while Rachel was beautiful in every way, modest, and yet vivacious. Leah caught Jacob's eye, but he had lost his heart to Rachel. So he said to his kinsman Laban: "I will stay and serve you for seven years for your younger daughter, Rachel." Now he did not tell Laban he could not go home, for he had stolen his brother's blessing. Laban was much impressed with Jacob's decision to remain with him. "Stay with me then," said Laban. "Since Rachel and you are of the same kinship group, it is better for her to marry you than a man outside our lineage." So Jacob served Laban for seven years, and they seemed to him like a handful of days because of his love for Rachel.

At last Jacob went to settle his account. "Give me Rachel as wife," he said to Laban, "for my time has been completed." He had waited seven years. So Laban prepared the wedding feast. He invited guests from the villages and towns. There was joy and celebration, with food and song and dancing and wine. Rachel herself was reticent, but often that is the way with brides. Laban made certain that Jacob's cup was never lacking wine. In the evening, Laban sent Jacob ahead to prepare the bridal chamber. "Be sure it is dark," he said to him, "for my youngest one is shy. I myself will bring her to you. In our country, that is our way." So Jacob retired to his marriage bed, and Laban led his daughter to him, kissed her, and went away. The girl lay down with Rebekah's son, quietly, there in the darkness. Jacob lifted her veil to kiss her, and he took her for his wife.

In the morning, just after dawn, as their room was filling with daylight, Jacob awoke, turned to his wife, and saw that it was Leah. What he said to her has not been recorded, but he said this to Laban. "Why, why have you done this to me? Why have you deceived me? Did I not ask for Rachel? Have I not labored for seven years for Rachel, whom I love?" Laban tried to calm him. "It is not our custom to marry the younger before the firstborn is wed," he replied. "Complete the wedding week with Leah, and you may have Rachel also, if you stay for seven more years." Now Laban knew there were no other males in their kinship group for Leah. He also knew that this was a way to keep Jacob in his service, and to keep his daughters together, and to keep them here at home. So Jacob remained a week with Leah, then he took Rachel as his wife. Jacob gladly worked for Laban for another seven years, so great was his love for Rachel.

Jacob gave to Rachel, the night that he first lay with her, his mother's *teraphim*. He blessed Bethuel's granddaughter, saying: "May Shaddai bless you and make you fruitful. May the blessings of Sarah descend through you from generation to generation." Rachel hid her *teraphim*, even from her sister. Although these treasures were rightfully hers as the youngest of the daughters and she alone had responsibility for continuing their kinship line, she did not wish to make Leah envious. She knew her sister was sad at heart, for although Jacob often slept with Leah, he loved Rachel best of all.

One day Laban saw Rachel's *teraphim* at the spring rites led by the women. He thought of his mother, Bethuel, and his grandmother Milcah, for these had been handed down to them and then given to Rebekah. Now the *teraphim* were home again. He took the treasures from Rachel, insisting they were the household gods and therefore rightfully his. He displayed the *teraphim* prominently, convinced that the gods would favor him for as long as he kept them there.

Leah conceived and gave birth to a son, and she named her firstborn Reuben, saying: "Godde has seen my affliction. Surely now my husband will love me." She conceived again and bore a son. "Godde heard that I am the lesser loved and gave me a second son," she said, and she named the baby Simeon. Again she conceived and again bore a son, saying, "Now my husband will be bound to me, for I have given him three sons." She named her third child Levi. Once more she conceived, and when she gave birth, she named her fourth son Judah, saying: "For this I give praise to Godde." Then Leah stopped bearing children.

✧ Bilhah and Zilpah

Laban had given gifts to his daughters at the time the two were wed. He gave Zilpah to Leah and Bilhah to Rachel to serve as their personal maids. Rachel also had Deborah, her nursemaid from birth, who had cared for and loved this motherless child as if she had been her own. Laban's wife had died in childbirth, and when the girls were growing up and a dispute would arise between them, Leah would remind Rachel that it was only because of her difficult birth that they had lost their mother. As sisters the two got along quite well, for they shared more than a husband. Despite a recurring rivalry, they remained the best of friends.

Now Leah, who felt unloved, was fertile, but her sister, Rachel, was barren, or so it would appear. Conscious that it was up to her to continue her kinship line, she said one night to Jacob, "Give me children or I shall die!" She meant, my lineage will perish if I do not produce an heir. "Do you think I am God?" Jacob shouted, angry at the suggestion that he might be to blame. "You are the one who is childless," he said. "Godde alone has withheld from you the fruitfulness of the womb." Then Jacob held her close that night and lay with her for many a night, but failed to bring life to her womb. Then Rachel did what women have done for countless generations when they have found they are not with child. "Sleep with Bilhah, my maid," she said, "that she might give birth to a child on my lap and I will have children through her." So Jacob took Bilhah to bed as wife, or perhaps as concubine, and Bilhah conceived and bore a son, and Rachel named him Dan. "Godde has heard my cry and judged me worthy of a son," she said, all the while rejoicing. Jacob slept with Bilhah again, and once again she was pregnant. When she gave birth to a second son, Rachel named him Naphtali. "I have fought

God's fight with my sister and won" is the meaning of that name.

Now Leah had ceased bearing children, so she went and did as her sister had done and gave her maid to Jacob. Jacob took Zilpah to bed as wife, some say as concubine, and she too conceived and bore a son whom Leah named "Good fortune!" by calling the baby Gad. Again, Jacob took Zilpah to bed and made the woman pregnant. "Happy am I," said Leah, "for women will call me happy," as Zilpah gave birth to a second son whom Leah named Asher in honor of Asherah.

✧ Rachel's Pregnancy

It was during the days of the wheat harvest, when the women and children were out in the fields, that Reuben found some mandrakes, purple flowers with thick roots known for medicinal magic. Rachel watched as the little boy gave the flowers to his mother. "Please give me some of those mandrakes," said Rachel, but her sister replied in anger, "You have taken away my husband. Must you have my mandrakes as well?" For Jacob no longer came to Leah as a husband to his wife, but spent the nights with Rachel to ease the pain of her barrenness. "Jacob can sleep with you tonight," said Rachel to her sister, "if you give me some of your mandrakes." She thought perhaps their magic might awaken fertility. When Jacob came in from the fields that evening, Leah called to her husband. "You must come and sleep with me tonight, for I have hired you with my mandrakes." So Jacob slept with Leah that night, and she conceived, and when it was time, gave birth to a fifth son, Issachar, meaning, "Godde has paid me my wages because I have given my maid to my husband." Jacob returned to Leah's tent. She conceived again and gave birth to a son, saying, "God has given me a fine dowry; now my husband will honor me, for I have given him six sons." She named the baby Zebulun. Jacob continued to visit Leah, and she gave birth to a seventh child, a little girl named Dinah. She was the last of Leah's children, perhaps because her husband did not sleep with her again.

Then Godde remembered Rachel. S/HE opened her womb, and Rachel joyfully awaited motherhood. "S/HE has taken away my shame," she cried, as she held her newborn baby. She named the boy Joseph, saying: "Godde, give me another one!"

✧ Migration to Canaan _____

After Rachel had given birth to Joseph and before the child was weaned, Jacob went into Laban and said, "Give me leave to return to my country and to my family's home. Let me take my wives and my children. I have served you faithfully all these years, and I can stay no longer." Jacob was eager to return to Canaan to claim his inheritance.

"I have been blessed because of you," said Laban. "My cattle, my children, all have prospered. How shall I repay you?" Jacob responded to Laban. "Indeed, you have fared well while I was here, for the little you had before I came has increased abundantly. But now I must be on my own to provide for my own household." "What shall I pay you," Laban asked, "for all your years of service?" "Pay me nothing," Jacob replied. "I did not work for wages. However, you can do this for me. Let me take from your flocks the speckled lambs and spotted sheep and the black lambs, there are so few, and the same from among your flocks of goats, and these shall be my wages." "Good!" said Laban. "It shall be so." But he was only pretending. He went and removed from all of his herds every speckled and spotted and black lamb, every speckled and spotted and black kid, and he gave these into the care of his sons, sending them off to pasture three days journey from Haran. All the rest of Laban's flocks remained in Jacob's care.

Now Jacob had been prepared for this, so before he had gone to Laban, he had secretly removed the strongest and best of the black and spotted animals and hidden them in a valley to the other side of Haran. Laban never suspected that Joseph was breeding a prize herd of speckled and spotted animals from the choicest of his flocks. The herd increased until Joseph had acquired a wealth of livestock to take with him when he left Paddan-aram. When Laban discovered Jacob's deceit, his sons were furious. "He has stolen our inheritance," they said. "He bred the flocks of our father. Those herds belong to us!"

✧ Rachel's *Teraphim* _____

Jacob decided it was time to leave. He took Rachel and Leah into the fields to where his flock was grazing and showed them what he had done. "Your father is ill disposed toward me because I have claimed what is my due. You know that I served him faithfully, yet time and again he cheated me. Ten times he changed my wages, then took the livestock he had promised me, yet the God of my people is with me. God's angel came to me in a dream and showed me how to seek redress. God said to me, 'I am Shaddai, the Godde of Beth-el, where you made a monument and a vow. Return now to the land of your birth. I will be with you always.'"

Rachel and Leah were deeply distressed with the deceptions of their father. "What inheritance is there for us here?" they said, for in matrilinear households, daughters do inherit. "He sold us to you," they said to Jacob, who indeed had paid their bride price with his service and with gifts. "Our father used the money to enrich himself, the money that was meant for us. What Godde has given to you belongs to us and to our children. Do as Godde has directed you. Our father considers us foreigners now. We will go with you." So Jacob set his wives and children on a caravan of camels, put all his possessions in wagons drawn by oxen or on donkeys' backs, assembled his herd of livestock, and with all he had acquired, departed for the land of Canaan to return to his family home.

Now Laban had gone to shear his sheep when Rachel slipped into his room and took his "household gods." Delighted to have her *teraphim* back, she wrapped them carefully, hid them away, and left her father's house. Three days had passed before Laban discovered that Jacob and his daughters were gone. Jacob had said nothing to Laban, for he knew he would never be allowed to leave with his wives and all their children. Laban, joined by his servants and sons, went in pursuit of Jacob. They traveled hard for seven days. Jacob had crossed the Euphrates and was entering the hills of Gilead when Laban caught up with him. He decided to wait until morning. Then God warned Laban in a dream, saying: "Not one harsh word to Jacob."

When Laban approached Jacob, he said, "Why have you deceived me? Why have you carried my daughters away like captives under the sword? Why did you flee in secret? I would have sent you away with song, with tambourines and dancing. I would have kissed my daughters goodbye and bid farewell to their children. What you have done is foolish. I have the power to harm you, but the God of your people prevented me from raising my hand against you. You left because you were longing for home, but why steal my household gods?" Then Jacob answered Laban. "We left in secret because I was afraid you would take my wives from me by force. We do not have your household gods. See for yourself. If you should happen to find them, whoever has them is yours." Now Jacob had no idea that Rachel had retrieved her *teraphim*. So Laban searched for his household gods, first Jacob's tent, then Leah's tent, then the tents of all their servants and maids, but he did not find them there. He came at last to Rachel's tent. Now Rachel had taken her *teraphim* and put them in the camel's saddle. She was sitting on the saddle when her father entered her tent. "Forgive me, father," she said to him, "for I cannot rise to greet you. It is now my time of month." Laban searched everywhere in the tent, everywhere but the saddle, and he found no household gods.

Jacob was angry with Laban. He said, "What is it that I have done to you? What is my offense? Look how you have pursued me and have searched through all my goods. What have you found that belongs to you? For twenty years I lived with you and cared for your flocks and cattle. I never ate a ram of your flock. No ewe or goat miscarried. If one of the herd was destroyed by beasts, I bore the loss myself. The heat of the day consumed me. Cold kept me awake at night. For twenty years I worked for you, worked fourteen years for your daughters, and six years for my flock. Ten times you changed my wages. If God had not been with me, I would have nothing now. The God who saw my affliction reprimanded you last night."

Then Laban said to Jacob, "The daughters are my daughters, the children are my children, the flocks are all my flocks. All that you have is mine. But what am I to do with these daughters of mine, or their children whom they have borne? Come, let us be at peace, you and I, for the sake of our children's children." So Jacob and Laban parted in peace. Laban kissed his children and grandchildren and early in the morning returned to Paddan-aram.

✧ Jacob Meets Esau _____

Now Jacob knew that his brother Esau might seek to do him harm. So he sent messengers ahead of them, that they might say to Esau, "Jacob who lived with Laban as an alien in the land is returning now to Canaan and begs to find favor with you." The messengers returned to Jacob, saying, "We saw Esau at a distance. It seems he is coming to meet you with a large mob of men." Jacob was fearful and distressed. He divided his caravan in two, forming two companies of women and children, flocks and herds, servants and herdsmen and cattle, thinking: "If Esau destroys one company, the other might escape."

Jacob sent gifts to Esau, sheep and goats, ewes and rams, camels and colts, cows and bulls, and male and female donkeys. He sent these ahead with his servants, so that each would arrive a drove at a time, with the following words to be spoken: "Here is a gift for Esau. It is from your servant Jacob, who is following close behind." Perhaps the gifts would appease his wrath before Jacob had to face him.

Jacob took his twelve children and the mothers of his children, and together with everything he had, he crossed the river Jabbock, a stream that, to the south of them, flowed into the river Jordan. They set up camp and stayed the night. Jacob went off to be alone and wrestled with himself until morning. Whether dream or vision or temptation to despair, Jacob fought a nameless terror in a struggle so intense that the muscle of his hip contracted and he had to limp away. As the sun rose, Jacob broke camp. Convinced he had wrestled with an angel, he said: "I have seen the face of God."

Jacob looked up and saw Esau approaching with a company of men, more than could be counted. So he lined up his wives and children, first Zilpah and her sons, then Bilhah with her sons, Leah with her sons and daughter, and last of all Rachel with Joseph. He bid them wait until he went ahead and met with his brother, Esau. Approaching his brother, he bowed seven times, as Esau ran to meet him. He embraced Jacob and kissed him, and he fell on his neck, and they wept. Esau looked up and said, "Who are these?" as Jacob's family drew near them. "The children whom God has graciously given," said Jacob to his brother. Then Zilpah approached, and Bilhah approached, and they bowed low, they and their children. Leah approached with her daughter and sons, and they too bowed before Esau. Finally, Rachel and Joseph arrived and bowed before Jacob's brother.

Esau did not know how to respond, so he turned to Jacob and asked, "What were those companies of cattle I met?" "They are a gift for you," said Jacob, "that I might find favor with you." But Esau said, "I have enough, my brother. Keep what you have for yourself." But Jacob urged his brother, saying, "Please, keep the gift I have sent to you. I will know that I have found favor with you, if you take this gift from my hand. You have received me so graciously, that truly, for me to see your face is like seeing the face of God. Please, accept this token, for God has been gracious to me." So Esau agreed. He said to Jacob, "Let us journey together, side by side." But Jacob quickly responded, "The children are young, the flocks are tired, and some of the lambs are nursing. If I overdrive them for even a day, I fear that the flocks may die. You go ahead, and I will follow, pacing myself to the animals and to the needs of my children. I will see you again in Seir." Esau agreed and departed.

Jacob journeyed westward until he came to Succoth. They stayed at Succoth for a while in tents, and then moved on to Shechem and decided to settle there. It was never meant to be permanent. Jacob wanted to take some time before going down to Hebron to claim his family home and the fields at Kiriath-arba, which were his inheritance. If he went too soon, Esau might recall his betrayal and seek revenge. It was better not to hurry. There were pasturelands at Shechem that were the envy of the Negeb. One day, when his boys were older, father and sons would return to Hebron and take up residence there.

✧ Dinah

Now Dinah, Leah's daughter, had grown into a lovely young girl of an age when men take notice. One day she went out from her mother's tent to visit some friends in the village. Spring was all around her. Women, here and there, were rehearsing the songs for the sowing of seeds and the blessing of crops in the rituals of planting.

As she walked along the path that led through the valley into the village, Shechem son of Hamor, son of a ruling family that long ago had given the village its name, overtook her and took hold of her to satisfy his passion, for he desired her. He drew her into the bushes where he lay with her by force. Dinah wept in anger and pain, but he spoke tenderly to her, seeking to comfort her. His heart had been drawn to Dinah. He said he wanted to marry her and that he loved her very much.

Dinah went home to her mother, who went and told her father, and he was wild with rage. He would not look on Dinah. He did not say a word. He would wait until his sons returned from their sojourn seeking pasture. Dinah, meanwhile, did not bleed, and before long it was certain. She was carrying Shechem's child. The women kept her secret and consulted their *teraphim.*

Shechem had tried to speak with Dinah without her father's knowledge. He slipped into the camp one day, and Rachel arranged a meeting. Later she told her sister that Shechem really loved her daughter and that the girl had forgiven him. Dinah would lie with him again, without her mother's knowledge, for her heart was drawn to Shechem, and she loved him very much.

Jacob's sons returned home. Dinah hid in terror, as loud voices rose from the tents long into the night. Now Shechem had said to his father, "Get me Dinah for my wife." Hamor had met with Jacob, saying, "The heart of my son longs for your daughter. Please give her to him in marriage. Put the marriage gift as high as you like, add more as reparation. Whatever you ask for, I will give, only give her as wife for Shechem." Now Jacob had been considering this, for it seemed a reasonable offer, since the damage had been done. He had said he would seek advice from his sons before he would set the penalty for violating his daughter, but when he mentioned this to them, they would not hear of it. "Should our sister be treated like a whore?" they shouted. And they argued, and they disagreed, and then they retired for the night.

Before dawn, while it was dark, Simeon and Levi left their tents and went to the home of Shechem. There they killed him with a sword to avenge their sister's honor. Since this was the way justice was done in those days in the land of Canaan, there was no further retribution. Jacob agonized over this sin and its stain upon his honor. "You have brought trouble to me," he said, for they were sojourners in Shechem, and he feared for his family's safety.

When Dinah heard what her brothers had done, she grieved greatly for many days and no one could console her. She continued to hide her pregnancy, and just when it was beginning to show, her mother Leah sent her away, to the home of Oholibamah, the youngest wife of Esau, who had once paid a visit to them, and she took the girl into her care. There Dinah married Korah, Oholibamah's son, and gave birth to a beautiful little girl whom Dinah named Tamar. It would be years before Dinah would ever see her father and brothers again.

✧ Jacob's Turning Point ⎯⎯⎯⎯⎯⎯⎯

Leah would have nothing to do with Jacob because of her daughter Dinah. She missed the girl, her lastborn, the family's only daughter. She grieved because she would not be there assisting at the birth of her grandchild, but she did not say this to Jacob. In time he might learn of Shechem's child, but it would never be from her. Jacob turned to Rachel for comfort. He too had suffered the loss of the girl who had touched his heart with her laughter and filled his days with delight. Losing her felt like the loss of Rebekah, and Rachel understood.

Soon after the departure of Dinah, Rachel found she was with child and praised Godde for the gift of life that lifted joy from sorrow. Jacob decided it was time to leave the territory of Shechem. They were no longer welcome there. People resented the violence that had been done to the son of Hamor, and they made life miserable for Jacob. He longed for the peace and security of his mother's trees and tents. He would return to Kiriath-arba to claim all that had been promised to him as his father's rightful heir.

They did not leave right away, for Rachel was feeling poorly, and the flocks were out to pasture. Then God appeared in a dream one night and spoke these words to Jacob: "Get up and go to Beth-el, and build an altar there, and atone for the life that was taken. I am El Shaddai." In the morning, Jacob was strangely troubled. He felt God was asking something of him, but he was at a loss to name it. That day, he ordered all of his household to give him their *teraphim*. This was the cause of his trouble, he said, for had he not lost a daughter? Had not the whole town turned against them? Did they not hear Rachel weeping, fearful she might lose her child? God seemed to be saying, get rid of these things, and Jacob was determined to obey. "Put away your foreign gods," said Jacob, "and let us go down to Beth-el, that I may make an altar there to the God who was with me in my distress and is with me wherever I go." So the women gave up their clay figurines, their religious talismans, and their assorted ritual objects, and Jacob took and buried them under the sacred oak in Shechem, for he still respected, and even feared, the power of the *teraphim* and the existence of other gods. Then Jacob, with his household and with all his flocks and possessions, pulled up stakes in Shechem and began the journey home. Now Rachel had never said to Jacob, "Here are my *teraphim*." She never told Jacob where she had put them, and Jacob never asked.

In due time they arrived at Beth-el, which is on the way to Hebron, and stopped to worship there. God appeared to Jacob again, saying to him in a dream, "You shall be a nation, a company of nations descended from your sons." Then Jacob called his sons together, the six sons of Leah, who are Reuben, Simeon, Levi, Judah, Issachar, and Zebulun; the two sons of Bilhah, Dan and Naphtali; and the two sons of Zilpah, whose names are Gad and Asher; but not Rachel's son. There at Beth-el they were circumcised, Jacob and his ten sons, and their blood was spilled upon the altar he had built there to worship God. They spent the time of their confinement recalling the deeds of their ancestors, how God had led their father Abraham into a land of promise, how God's covenant blessings flowed through those who were signed with the covenant, which had been sealed with their blood, and how the firstborn male among them would inherit from this day on. Now Rachel kept Joseph close to her and cradled him on her lap. Her time was fast approaching. She rejoiced to feel life leap in her womb, even as she beheld her cherished traditions falling away. Jacob, because of his love for Rachel and because she had resisted, did not put the knife to Joseph, who was still a little boy.

✧ Rachel's Legacy ⎯⎯⎯⎯⎯⎯⎯⎯⎯⎯⎯⎯⎯⎯⎯⎯⎯

From Beth-el they journeyed south again. They had scarcely left the area when Deborah, Rachel's nursemaid, weary with age and the pain of life, lay down on her mat and died. They buried her under a large oak tree just below Beth-el, and Rachel mourned for her there. Her death was a sign of things to come.

They had been on the road for less than a month and were approaching the town of Ephrath, later known as Bethlehem, when Rachel went into labor. Her delivery was difficult. After long hours of hard labor, her midwife said to her, "Do not be afraid. There is life in you. You are giving birth to a son." But Rachel would not survive. She put her child to the breast of another, as her mother had done before her. Clutching her sacred *teraphim,* she named her baby Ben-oni, "son of my suffering." Shortly after, she died.

Jacob buried Rachel by the side of the road, under the shade of a flowering tree whose blossoms were thick and fragrant. He marked the grave with a pillar of stones, and there he mourned for her. Jacob planned to come back for Rachel, once he was settled in Hebron, to bring her bones to Machpelah to lay beside his mother. He always believed he would do this, through all those years of his very long life, but to this day, Rachel remains by the road near Bethlehem. Now when it was dark and all were asleep, Jacob returned to Rachel's grave, and there he buried her *teraphim,* carefully and gently, beside her. He did not know Leah was watching. When he left, Leah found the spot and dug them up again. She wrapped the *teraphim* in her shawl and then hid them away, telling no one, and quietly wept for Rachel.

On the eighth day after Rachel died giving birth to her son, Ben-oni, Jacob circumcised the boy and named him Benjamin.

Now before they arrived in Hebron, while they were still journeying through the land, Reuben, Leah's eldest son and, as firstborn, heir to Jacob, went and lay with Zilpah, his father's concubine, and Jacob heard of it. He said nothing to Reuben, but from that moment he dismissed him as heir to the covenant, which would pass to the younger yet again.

Jacob settled down in the land where his father had lived with his mother, where he had lived as a boy until he matured and then left to become a man. There Leah died and was laid to rest in the cave, beside Rebekah. Jacob never knew that before she died, she had given to Asher, Zilpah's youngest son, the *teraphim* of Rachel, and had made him promise to give them to

Dinah who had settled in Seir. Asher kept his promise. He went to visit his sister and was overjoyed to see her again and to meet her sons and daughters, not knowing that the elder girl was conceived of Shechem's seed. Dinah treasured the *teraphim,* which she handed on to her daughter, not to her youngest, as tradition holds, but to her eldest, Tamar, the child of her lost love.

✧ Rachel's Son Joseph _____

Joseph was seventeen years old, a shepherd, like his brothers. He was his father's favorite, for Jacob loved him best of all. The child of his old age, he would say, the child of his beloved Rachel, which made his brothers envious, even angry at times. Joseph had a long-sleeved garment, a robe of many colors given to him by his father to mark his coming of age, when he too had been circumcised, the last of Jacob's sons to be sealed with the sign. He wore the robe with a flourish, for his days were full of energy and his nights were filled with dreams.

Joseph took delight in recalling his dreams and sharing them with his brothers in the evening, under the stars. "I dreamed," said Joseph, "we were binding sheaves, all of us, in a field, when suddenly my sheaf stood upright, while your sheaves bowed low to the ground." "Who do you think you are?" they said. "Are you to reign over us? Seek dominion over us?" They hated him and his dreams. He shared another dream with them, saying, "The sun, the moon, and eleven stars were bowing down before me." "What kind of a dream is that?" they said, and even his father wondered. "Do you think we are going to bow down to you? That your father and brothers should submit to you?" And they hated him all the more. Jealous of him and tired of his talk, they dismissed his dreams as folly, but Jacob remembered them all.

Now his brothers had gone to pasture their flocks in an area south of Shechem, and Joseph had stayed behind. Recalling all that had happened there and the hostility of the people, Jacob sent for Joseph and said, "Find your brothers who are with the flocks, and see if all is well with them; then bring word back to me." So Joseph went up to Shechem and searched the hollows all around, but he did not find them there. A shepherd saw him wandering the fields. "Who are you seeking?" he asked him. "My brothers," Joseph responded. "They are here pasturing their flocks." The shepherd said, "I have seen them, but that was days ago. They were heading north toward Dothan." So Joseph went in search of his brothers, to ease the mind of his father, and eventually caught up with them.

They saw him from a distance, the brother who had supplanted them in the estimation of their father, his flashy robe a splash of color caught in the setting sun. "Here comes the dreamer," they said. "Let us be rid of him." They began to plot how this might be done. "Throw him into a pit," said one. "Only after we kill him," said another. "We can say wild animals devoured him. See then what becomes of his dreams." Reuben overheard their plans. "No more shedding of blood," he said, for he had not forgotten Shechem. "Get rid of him, but spare his life. Throw him into a pit here, out in the wilderness, but lay no hand on him, for he is our father's son." Now Reuben was hoping to rescue Joseph and restore him to their father and perhaps redress the wrong he had done in taking his concubine. When Joseph arrived, his brothers seized him and stripped him of his garment and threw him into an empty pit that was dry and very deep. Then they moved on with their flocks.

The next day some merchants who were passing by heard what sounded like a cry for help and went to investigate. There, in a pit, was Joseph. Then they saw a caravan approaching, one that belonged to traders who carry resin and balm to Egypt, so they rescued Joseph and then sold him to them for a handful of silver. The caravan continued on its way, and Joseph went down into Egypt.

Reuben, who had followed after the flocks, returned to find that the pit was empty and his heart was filled with dread. So he and his brothers slaughtered a goat, dipped Joseph's robe in the animal's blood, and brought it back to Jacob. "We found this," they said. "Isn't it Joseph's robe?" Jacob recognized the garment, torn and stained with blood. "It is Joseph's robe," he cried in despair, "a wild animal has devoured him and ripped his flesh to pieces." Then Jacob tore his garments. Night and day he mourned for Joseph, refusing to be comforted. They did what they could to console him, but Jacob said, "I shall go to my grave grieving for Rachel's son."

✧ Tamar

Judah had been the first to marry. He fell in love with a Canaanite woman he had met while both were pasturing their sheep. The woman's name was Shua. Judah married Shua and went to live in the hills near Adullam, not far from Shua's home. There he befriended a man named Hirah, who was also a keeper of sheep.

Shua conceived and bore a son and Judah named him Er. She conceived again and bore a son, whom she herself named Onan. She would give birth a third time, while in the village of Chezib, and when she delivered another boy, she named the baby Shelah. There are no records of other births, except in the memories of women, yet Shua was pregnant again, and again, and gave birth to beautiful daughters.

When Shua's oldest son was of age, his father arranged a marriage for him, for he was Judah's firstborn and a patriarch of the tradition. Er married Tamar, a lovely girl from another valley, and she made her home with him. Now Er was not easy to live with. He was often in trouble and had a reputation in the

town. One day he was involved in a vicious fight and was so
badly beaten he fell down and died. After the time of mourning had passed, Judah went to his son Onan, who had also come
of age and was preparing to take a wife. "It is your duty," he
said to his son, "to see to it there are offspring who are born
of your brother's wife." That was the code of the patriarch, that
a brother would take his deceased brother's wife and impreg-
nate her in his brother's name so she could give birth to his
heir. So Onan did as his father had asked, but Onan despised his
brother, and knowing the child would not be his own, he spilled
his semen outside of Tamar whenever he slept with her. He continued to sleep with Tamar, with no intention of her conceiving.
Tamar grieved and prayed to Godde to remove this humiliation.
Soon after, Onan fell ill with a fever, and before long, he also
died. Judah was overcome with grief and wondered who this
woman was who had cost him two of his sons. So after the time
of mourning had passed, he said to Tamar his daughter-in-law,
"Return to your family for a little while and remain a widow
in your father's house, until Shelah is ready to marry," for he
knew he was obliged to give him to her, yet he feared for his
young son's safety, and Shelah was the last of his sons. So Tamar
went home to her mother, to live as a widow in her father's care
until Judah sent for her.

Time passed, and Shua died. Judah mourned for Shua his
wife, the mother of his children, and when the time of mourning was over, he went up to Timnah to his sheepshearers,
accompanied by Hirah his friend. Now Tamar had waited a long,
long time for Judah to send for her. She knew, since Shelah was
of age by now, that Judah would not be returning. She, a widow
twice over, longing to have children, what was she to do?

It was her mother Dinah who counseled her. Together they
schemed and conceived a plan and awaited the appropriate
time. One day Dinah said to Tamar, "Your father-in law has gone
to Timnah for the shearing of his sheep." It was the appropriate
time. Tamar took off her widow's garments and traveled north
to Timnah. She wrapped herself in a robe and veil and sat down

at the crossroads, just outside of Enaim, which is on the road to Timnah. When Judah saw her sitting there, he thought she was a prostitute, so he went over to her at the side of the road and said, "Come, let me lie with you," for he felt the need for a woman. "What will you give me," she said to him, "if I let you lie with me?" He replied, "I will send you a kid from my flock." And she said, "You must give me some guarantee, a pledge to keep as security until you send it to me." He said, "What pledge shall I give you?" for he was not sure what she had in mind. "Your signet and your ring," she said, "and the staff that you are holding." So he gave them to her, and he lay with her, by the side of the road, in the bushes. Then he got up and went his way, unaware he had entered his daughter-in-law, for the thick veil that had hidden her face concealed her identity. Then Tamar removed the veil and the robe that signified a prostitute and returned home to her mother. She put on the garments of widowhood again, and in due time she discovered that at last she was with child.

Now Judah had asked his friend Hirah to take a kid from the flock to the woman and recover his pledge from her, but when Hirah went to look for her, he was unable to find her. He inquired of the townspeople, "Where is the ritual prostitute who was sitting by the wayside just outside of Enaim?" "No prostitute has been here," they said. So Hirah returned to Judah. "I have not been able to find her. There has been no prostitute there, they said, not yesterday, not ever. They told me I was mistaken." Then Judah replied, "Let it be. Let her keep the things I have given her, otherwise people will laugh at me, saying, 'You lay with her, you gave her a kid, and then you could not find her!'"

Three months later Judah was told that his daughter-in-law was pregnant. "Tamar has played the whore," they said. "You must send for her and destroy her." A delegation went to Tamar's house and brought back this word to Judah: "Who owns these made me pregnant." Then Judah was handed a signet and ring and a staff with his mark upon it. Judah acknowledged these and said, "She is more in the right than I am, for I did not give her Shelah, so she took what was hers from me." Tamar had sent some other items wrapped in a woven cloth. These too were handed to Judah. He opened the cloth, and there he saw his mother's *teraphim.*

Judah, twice taken by surprise, was far more startled by this second revelation and all that it implied. He rushed to the home of Tamar and embraced his sister Dinah, rejoicing that all was well with her, and that she was a wife and a mother. He was grateful that she had forgiven him for what had been done to her and to the man she had loved. Dinah never said so, but somehow he knew that the widow of his sons was her living link to Shechem. He returned the *teraphim* to Tamar and walked away from his sister's child, the mother of his sons. For yes, there were twins in Tamar's womb, and when it came time to bring to birth, one of the boys put out a hand while she labored to deliver. The midwife tied a crimson thread to it, saying, "This one came out first." But the hand drew back, and out came the brother. "What a breakthrough for you!" said the midwife, so he was named Perez. The second was born with a crimson thread, and Tamar named him Zerah. Tamar and Dinah raised the boys and surrounded them with love.

✧ Potiphar's Wife

Now Joseph, son of Rachel, was taken into Egypt by a caravan of traders and sold to an officer of Pharaoh, the captain of his guard, whose name was Potiphar. At first, Joseph was merely a slave who did his master's bidding, but he soon rose to the status of steward because of his efficiency. All that he did prospered, whether in the house or out in the fields, so that one day Potiphar put Joseph in charge of all he had. With Joseph there, he had no concerns, for the young man served him faithfully, ungrudgingly, and well.

Joseph was a good-looking man. Potiphar's wife was a beautiful woman. One day, when Potiphar was away and the servants were out on errands, Joseph approached his master's wife and said, "Let us lie together," for the day was warm, the trees in bud, and he was feeling like a man. Now the woman did not discourage him, for she found Joseph attractive and charmingly attentive, and Potiphar had been gone so long. So Joseph lay with Potiphar's wife, not once, but several times, but only when his master was away and all his servants gone.

Time passed, and Joseph was no longer drawn to dalliance with his mistress. He had noticed one of her chambermaids and imagined himself with her. One day, when his mistress said, "Come, lie with me," he refused, and she was angry, for this was how he had replied. "I cannot, for my master trusts me. He has given me charge of all he has, but certainly not his wife. If he discovers I have been with you, he will dismiss me from my position, and I will lose everything I have gained. I will not do it again." One other time she came to him, for she was filled with longing, and once again, he refused. "Lie with me," she pleaded with him, pulling off his garment as he ran out of the house. Now one of the servants who had returned heard the cry of her mistress and came running to her aid. "This despicable slave has insulted me," said the mistress, holding his garment. "He tried to force me to lie with him and was angry when I refused. He ran away when I shouted for help. See, here is his garment." And she continued to cry.

Potiphar returned later that day. His wife, clutching Joseph's garment, repeated her story, accusing Joseph with anger and with tears. Potiphar sent for Joseph and said, "So this is the way you have treated me, after I trusted you," and he became enraged. He sent Joseph to prison, where he remained for quite some time.

✧ Joseph the Dreamer _____

Joseph was placed in an area where Pharaoh's prisoners were confined. The chief jailer took a liking to Joseph and put him in charge of the others who were imprisoned there with him. The jailer could find no fault with Joseph, for he did everything well.

One day Pharaoh became angry with two officers of his court, his cupbearer and his chief baker, and he had them put into custody in the prison where Joseph was confined. One morning both of them woke with a dream, with no one to interpret, and they were sorely troubled. "Why so sad?" Joseph asked, and when he heard the reason he said, "Tell your dreams to me."

The cupbearer told this dream to Joseph. "There was a vine before me, and on the vine, three branches. As soon as it budded, blossoms came, and as quickly, clusters of grapes. Pharaoh's cup was in my hand. I pressed the ripe grapes into the cup and gave the cup to Pharaoh." Joseph gave this interpretation. "The three branches are three days. In three days Pharaoh will restore you to your office, and you shall place his cup in his hand, just as you did before." The cupbearer was delighted. Then Joseph said to the cupbearer, "Remember me when it is well with you. Make mention of me to Pharaoh, that I might be free of this place."

When the chief baker heard such a favorable interpretation, he was happy to tell his dream. "I also had a dream," he said. "There were three bread baskets on my head. The uppermost basket was filled with all kinds of baked delights for Pharaoh, but the birds were eating out of this basket that was on the top of my head." Joseph gave this interpretation. "The three baskets are three days. In three days Pharaoh will take you by the head and hang you from a pole, and the birds will eat your flesh."

On the third day, Pharaoh's birthday, he held a feast, and at that time he restored the chief cupbearer; but he hung the chief baker on a pole, as Joseph had predicted. The chief cupbearer returned to his task and forgot to remember Joseph.

Two years later, Pharaoh dreamed he was standing by the Nile, when seven cows, healthy and fat, came up out of the river and were grazing in the grass. Then seven more cows, ugly and thin, swallowed the other ones. With that, Pharaoh awoke. He fell asleep again and dreamed a second time. Seven ears of grain, plump and fine, were growing on a single stalk. Then seven other ears, blighted and thin, sprouted up after them. The thin ears swallowed the seven plump ears. That was Pharaoh's dream. He awoke and sent for magicians and sages, for he was deeply troubled; but when he told his dreams to them, none could interpret them. Suddenly his chief cupbearer recalled a man by the name of Joseph who was in Pharaoh's prison and could interpret dreams. He told how Joseph had heard his dream and that of the chief baker, and had said one would be restored to office while the other would be hanged, and that he had been right.

So Pharaoh sent for Joseph, and he was brought up from the dungeon. He bathed, put on clean clothes, and went into the presence of Pharaoh. "I have had a dream," Pharaoh said, "and there is none to interpret. I need someone to discern for me, and they say you are the one." Then he told his dreams to Joseph, who spoke these words to Pharaoh. "The two dreams are one and the same. The cows, the ears, are seven good years, years of bountiful harvests. The seven lean cows, the seven lean ears, are years of devastating famine that will follow a time of plenty. The situation will be so severe that abundance will be forgotten as drought consumes the land. God has revealed what will come to pass. The doubling of the dream is a sure sign it has been confirmed by God."

Pharaoh, shaken by these words, heard this advice from Joseph. "Let Pharaoh select one who is wise and discerning and set him over the land of Egypt to prepare for what is to come. Let overseers be appointed to collect one-fifth of all the harvest during the years of plenty. Let food and grain be gathered under the authority of Pharaoh and reserves of grain collected and stored, so that there will be food for the cities when disaster befalls the land, lest the people perish."

The proposal made sense to Pharaoh. He was pleased with all that Joseph had said. "You are the one I have chosen," he said, looking straight at Joseph. "I put you in charge of my store-houses. You will be second only to me." Then he placed a ring on his finger, put a gold chain around his neck, gave him some regal garments, and had him ride in a chariot designated for Pharaoh's second-in-command.

✧ Asenath

Pharaoh also gave Joseph a wife. She was Asenath, daughter of Potiphera, the high priest of On, whose mother was a priestess, and some say, so was she, for the name Asenath means "servant of the goddess," or "belonging to the goddess." Pharaoh gave Joseph a new name, Zaphenath-paneah, meaning "the god speaks and the one who bears the name listens."

So Joseph became an Egyptian, in name, demeanor, and all other ways, as reflected in the names of his children, which announce his embrace of the cultural and religious heritage of his wife. Asenath gave birth to two sons before the years of famine, and Joseph called the firstborn Manasseh, meaning "God has made me forget all my hardship and all my father's house," and he named the younger Ephraim, which means "for God has made me fruitful in the land of my misfortunes."

There is no indication that Joseph ever took a wife other than Asenath. Her spiritual and religious practices surely reminded him of Rachel. Once again he could drink from the bountiful breast of S/HE who is Cosmic Mother or sit in the lap of his mother's Godde and be held in her embrace.

✧ Joseph the Provider ────────────────

Joseph traveled throughout Egypt, storing up grain in the cities, stocking reserves in fields all around, so that grain was so abundant, piled high and wide like the sand of the sea, the amount could not be measured.

The years of plenty came to an end, just as Joseph had predicted, and the years of famine began. There was havoc in neighboring nations, but in Egypt there was bread. Whenever the people were hungry, whenever they cried out to Pharaoh, he said to them: "Go to Joseph. Whatever he tells you, do." Joseph opened the storehouses and sold grain to the Egyptians, for the shortages were severe. People of other nations came to Egypt to barter for food, for the famine was widespread. Everywhere food was scarce, but Joseph was prepared.

When Jacob heard there was grain in Egypt, he said to his sons, "Go, buy grain, or we will surely die." So his sons went down to Egypt, all but Benjamin. They came face to face with Joseph and bowed low to the ground, and Joseph remembered his dream. He recognized his brothers, but they did not know who he was. "Who are you?" Joseph inquired of them. "We are twelve brothers, sons of one man. The youngest is with his father, and one of us is no more." Then Joseph gave them grain, saying, "Do not return to me again without your youngest brother."

They left Egypt laden with grain, but when they stopped for lodging that night, one of them found the money he had paid lying there in his sack. So it was for all the others, money in each of their sacks, and they were confused and afraid. They returned to their home, ate the grain, and once again were hungry.

Then Jacob said, "Return to Egypt, for all our rations are gone." "Not without our brother," they replied, "for we were warned not to return unless Benjamin came with us." Jacob would not consent to this. "Why did you tell him so many things? Why say you had another brother?" "The man asked many questions," they said. "How were we to know?" Jacob was distraught. "This boy will not go down with you. I have already lost his brother. I will not risk losing him. What if something should happen? Then I should surely die." His sons steadfastly refused to go. Then Judah said, "Send the boy with me. I will stake my life on his safety. If I do not bring him back to you, let your judgment fall on me. Now let us go and secure some food, or all of us will die. We could have been there and back by now. Let us be on our way." With that, Jacob relented. He sent with them gifts from Canaan, such as balm, resin, pistachios, a little honey, and some almonds. He told them to take extra money with them, double the amount required, and to return what was found in their sacks. So off they went to Egypt, with extra money, an offering of gifts, and their brother Benjamin.

When Joseph caught sight of Benjamin, he instructed his chief steward, saying, "Invite the men to my house. They will dine with me at noon." As they were led into Joseph's house, the brothers became alarmed. "Why are we here?" they asked one another. "It must be the money we found in our sacks! They will say it was stolen. They will charge us with theft. They will make slaves out of us." They began to explain to the steward that it was all a big mistake, that they had not put the money there, that they had come back to return it, but the steward said, "Do not be concerned," and brought water to wash their feet.

When Joseph arrived they presented their gifts, and he asked about their father. He saw his brother Benjamin and said, "So this is the brother of whom you spoke," and then he left the room quite suddenly, because he was moved to tears on seeing his mother's son. He composed himself, returned to the hall, and told them all to be seated, arranging the brothers in their birth order from the eldest down to the youngest. They saw this and were amazed. Joseph sat apart from them, for custom forbid Egyptians to eat with people of their kind, but he saw to it that Benjamin's portion was five times that of his brothers. They ate and drank and got happily drunk, rejoicing in their good fortune. Then they retired for the night.

At sunrise they departed, the donkeys straining beneath their loads, for they had many bags of grain, enough for all their household. Meanwhile, Joseph instructed his steward to return their money to them as before and to hide his silver cup inside the sack of the youngest one. Once they are outside the city, he said, pursue and overtake them and demand they give back my silver cup, which I use for interpretation. The steward did as he was told, and the brothers were astounded. "Why would we return evil for good? Should you find the cup with anyone here, that person's life will be forfeit." Their sacks were searched, and there it was, inside the sack of Benjamin. The steward would have taken Benjamin, but his brothers would not allow it.

Terrified, all of them returned to the city and went into the presence of Joseph, who said, "What foolishness, this deed you have done. Did you not know that a man like me who practices interpretation can know more than you know?" They had fallen prostrate before him. Judah spoke on their behalf. "We are innocent of this crime," he said, "but how are we to prove it? Take all of us as your slaves." Joseph replied, "Only one of you is guilty. That one shall be my slave. The rest of you, return to your father." Then Judah spoke a second time. "I beg you, take me in place of the boy, for he is the life of his father, the cherished child of his old age, whose deceased mother had two sons, and he alone survives. How could I go home to my father without bringing the boy with me? He would surely die." With that, Joseph cleared the room of all but himself and his brothers, and he revealed himself to them. "I am Joseph," he said, breaking into sobs. "Is my father still alive?" His brothers stood there, absolutely stunned, unable to utter a word. He repeated, "I am your brother Joseph." He embraced Benjamin, kissed him and wept, and kissed every one of his brothers. There was an awkwardness at first, then suddenly, all of them spoke at once in a burst of raucous confusion heard all the way to Pharaoh's court. Joseph said, "Tell my father. Tell him how I am honored here. Tell him to come to me."

So they left Egypt for the land of Canaan and returned home to their father. "He is alive!" they said to him. "Joseph reigns in Egypt." Then they told of all that had happened to them, what they had seen and what they had heard, and they showed Jacob the wagons, saying, "Joseph sent these wagons so we might bring you down to Egypt." Jacob's spirit revived. "Enough!" he said. "My son is alive. I must see him before I die."

✧ Migration into Egypt _____

Jacob sent Judah ahead to Joseph to prepare for his arrival. He was not coming just to visit. He was bringing all of his family and would stay until the end of the famine, which was said to be years away. They were hoping to settle in Goshen, where other shepherds pastured flocks. They would be more comfortable there.

So Jacob went down to Egypt with his children, their children, husbands, wives, their livestock and all their possessions, to sojourn there in Goshen. Joseph harnessed his chariot and rode to meet his father. Who can describe their feelings of joy as Rachel's husband and Rachel's child embraced, wept, and praised her Godde, for surely S/HE was with them. "Now that my eyes have looked into your eyes, I can die in peace," said Jacob. Then Joseph went to Pharaoh and told him his family had arrived and that all of them were shepherds and would settle in the region of Goshen, which was where the shepherds lived, for in Egypt shepherds were considered to be of a lower class. So Joseph's people, with all of their livestock, settled in the land of Goshen.

Not a single crop could be harvested, for famine still gripped the land. People were hungry everywhere and their suffering was intense. Residents of Egypt and people from Canaan gave money to Joseph in exchange for grain, which he put into Pharaoh's treasury. When their money was gone, the Egyptians said, "Give us food or we will die. We have no money to give you." "Then give me your livestock," Joseph said, "and you will have food in exchange." So they brought their livestock to Joseph, their donkeys and horses, their flocks and herds, and he gave them food to last for a year, but after a year it was gone. They came again, saying to him, "Our money is spent, our herds are gone, we have only our land and our bodies. We have nothing else to give. Take us into your service, and we will work for bread." So Joseph gave seed and they sowed the seed, and gave Pharaoh one-fifth of their harvests, which continued beyond the famine as a statute in the land. During the time of famine, Joseph gained much for Pharaoh, took money and land and livestock and the services of the people, many of whom were enslaved. At first the people were grateful, for they had food enough to live. When the famine ended and circumstances changed, there was tension throughout the land.

The children of Rachel and Leah, the children of Zilpah and Bilhah, survived and prospered in Goshen, despite what they endured. Asher, Zilpah's younger son who was born of Leah's line, married a Goshen woman who gave birth to a daughter, Serah. She was the delight of everyone, giving life to Jacob in his old age. In her the descendants of matriarchs were no longer aliens in another land, but at home with a mix of traditions. Serah's religious practices, honoring her namesake Asherah, also the namesake of her father, stirred memories of Rachel and Leah, Rebekah and Sarah, and the faith of ancient times. It is not known quite how or when she acquired the *teraphim*. What we know is that all the women who had come into the land of Canaan kept company together, held festivals together, told stories to one another, and kept their traditions alive.

✧ Blessings

The time of Jacob's death drew near, and he called Joseph to him and said, "Bring me your sons, Rachel's sons, for your children are my children. Let me bless them before I die." So Joseph brought his sons to him. Jacob pulled them close and embraced them and prepared to give them his blessing. Now Ephraim was standing at the right hand of Jacob and Manasseh on the left. Joseph switched them around so that his firstborn would be on the right. Then Jacob stretched out his right hand and placed it on the head of Ephraim, who was standing to his left, and placed his left hand on Manasseh's head. Joseph, aghast, said to his father, "The firstborn is here, on your right." Jacob quietly responded, "I know, my son, I know." Then the patriarch, husband and son of matriarchs, who had usurped a firstborn's blessing, who loved his younger sons best of all, blessed Rachel's grandchildren, favoring the younger one. Jacob remembered Rachel, the younger daughter, and smiled.

Jacob gathered his family around him and blessed every one of his children and every one of their children. He reserved for Judah, Leah's younger son, the responsibility of continuing the covenant of Abraham and Isaac. Judah would also be a patriarch strongly influenced by matriarchs and would continue both those lines. Then Jacob blessed Dinah and her daughters, saying:

> By the Godde of your mother who will help you,
> by Shekinah Shaddai who will bless you
> > with blessings from above
> > and blessings of the deep,
> > blessings of the breasts and of the womb,
> so shall your blessings be.

The blessings of S/HE Who Is are like
    the blessings of the eternal mountains,
    and the bounties of the everlasting hills.

✧ Death and Burial of Rebekah's Son Jacob ───────────

Then Jacob charged his sons, saying, "Bury me with my ancestors, in the cave in the field of Machpelah, under the oaks of Mamre, in the place where I buried Leah. Lay me down beside her, with my father, Isaac, and my mother, Rebekah, with Abraham and with Sarah." Just as he was breathing his last, he whispered the name "Rachel." So Jacob died and was gathered to his people, and many mourned for him.

Joseph had his father embalmed, for this was Egyptian practice. It was done by their physicians, and it took them many days. Then Joseph went to Pharaoh and said, "Let me go and bury my father in Canaan, as I had promised him," and Pharaoh gave his permission, saying to Joseph, "Fulfill your vow." So they went up to Canaan, all of Jacob's household except the livestock and little children, with representatives of Pharaoh, with chariots and horsemen accompanying them, a very large delegation. Then just beyond the Jordan, they stopped at a place called Atad and spent seven days mourning Jacob with loud lamentation. After they had buried Jacob with his people in Kiriath-arba, they went back down to Egypt and continued residence there.

✧ Death and Burial of Rachel's Son Joseph

Joseph died in Egypt. His body was embalmed and his bones interred in a crypt that was given by Pharaoh. Asenath, who lived much longer than he, gave the burial blessing and then went to mourn her husband at the temple in Heliopolis.

Joseph had seen his children's children, but he did not live to see and face the consequences of what he had done. He had helped his people survive the famine as sojourners in Egypt, but he had also set in motion a process whereby they and their descendants would eventually be enslaved. Asenath, as priest to a large and liberated circle of Egyptian women, did what she could to alleviate the distress of the lower class. Her granddaughter Sheerah, Ephraim's child, who was raised in the tradition of matriarchs, was a leader too, like her grandparents. She struggled on behalf of her people, raising awareness among the oppressed to the injustices of Pharaoh and the right to control their lives. Her spiritual counsel and inherent wisdom were sought after far and wide. Through her the ancient rupture between the ancestors, Jacob and Esau, was finally faced and forgiven. Healing had come to both sides through the patient prayers of women, especially Sheerah and her elder, Timnah, concubine to Eliphaz, son of Adah, Esau's Canaanite wife.

✧ Midwives and Mothers _____

Joseph's brothers and sister died. So did that whole generation of those who had followed him to Egypt and who had thrown in their lot with him. Then their children died, and their grandchildren. Many never knew or had forgotten why they had ever left the land their ancestors had chosen to dwell in, although some of the elders among them still spoke of Canaan as home. Even to those elders who kept the tradition, Canaan was a distant memory, Egypt a present reality difficult to endure.

The people who came to be known as Hebrews because of ethnic similarities and genealogical bonds grew in number in Egypt. This was cause for concern to those who would keep them under control.

Now a new king arose in Egypt who did not know Joseph and had not a shred of empathy for his descendants and their kind. He conscripted their men into service, imposing tasks with a ruthlessness that made their lives bitter and their suffering severe. It is said the cities were built with their sweat, that the rivers ran with their tears. None escaped the oppression, neither the women nor their children. Nearly everyone dreamed of freedom, but few dared speak it aloud.

Pharaoh was determined to stem the spread of this blight upon his dynasty. Lower the number of able-bodied males, this was his solution, for he knew the people were restless and he feared they might take up arms. "They are a plague on my house," he would say to the officers in command. So he summoned Shiprah and Puah, two of the Hebrew midwives who were leaders among the others and whose skills were such they were sometimes called to assist Egyptian women. They had delivered Pharaoh's daughter. He knew them to be intelligent women capable of convincing others. "Tell the midwives of Hebrew women what Pharaoh has decreed," he said. "When a boy is born, kill him. Throw him into the Nile. If a girl, you may let her live."

Shiprah and Puah did no such thing, nor did any of the other midwives. The women gave birth to daughters and sons and all were allowed to flourish. Pharaoh summoned the two again, and other midwives with them. "Why have you ignored my order and allowed the boys to live?" he shouted. "Because Hebrew women are hard-working women and strong, not like Egyptians. They give birth to their children easily and deliver them on their own, before the midwife arrives." There was nothing Pharaoh could say or do in response to that reply. Women gave birth, and their numbers increased; even the midwives had families, for Godde was protecting them. Then Pharaoh decreed to his own people, "Should you hear that a boy is born to the Hebrews, throw the baby into the Nile, but let the girls live."

✧ Daughters

A Levite woman born in Egypt whose name was Jochebed married Amram, her brother's son. A strong priestly tradition distinguished their matrilineal line, a quality both had inherited and would pass on to their daughter and sons.

Jochebed gave birth to a baby girl and named her Miriam. Her second child was a boy born before the decree of Pharaoh. Aaron was his name. She conceived a third time and bore a son and her heart was filled with anguish, for the authorities were watching Hebrew women and killing their newborn boys. "How beautiful my baby," she would say, as she concealed him from all but her family for three terrifying months. When she could hide no longer, for it was known she had given birth, she and her daughter, an inventive child, conceived a daring plan.

Jochebed wove a papyrus basket and sealed it with a sticky substance called bitumen, or pitch. She put her baby in the basket and set the basket among the reeds on the bank along the river. Her daughter Miriam hid at a distance, keeping watch over her brother to see what would happen to him. Pharaoh's daughter, as was her custom, came down to the river to bathe, accompanied by her maids. As her attendants strolled along the banks and she was in the water, she saw a basket among the reeds and sent her maid to get it. She unwrapped the cloth and saw a baby who was just beginning to cry. "Could this be one of the Hebrew children?" she asked. Her heart was drawn to the child. She had tried to convince her father to give up his evil plan, for she had been delivered by a Hebrew, but all he would do, on her behalf, was exempt girls from the decree.

Now the baby in the basket could have been anybody's baby, so Pharaoh's daughter reasoned, for the boy was uncircumcised. The child lacked the Hebrew sign, so how would her father know? She could say the boy was Egyptian, that his mother had died while giving birth and the family had abandoned him. "I will keep this baby," she said to her maids. "I will raise him as my own." Then Miriam ran to where they stood and said to Pharaoh's daughter, "What a beautiful baby you have found. Do you need someone to nurse it? My mother can, she just lost a child. Shall I bring her here to you?" "Yes," said Pharaoh's daughter. So the little girl ran to get Jochebed, who hurried to Pharaoh's daughter. "Take this child and nurse it for me," she said to the baby's mother, "and I will pay your wages." Then Pharaoh's daughter named the baby, calling the little boy Moses, "because I drew him out of the water."

Jochebed took her baby home and nursed the boy for wages that were paid from Pharaoh's account. When her son was weaned, though it broke her heart, she and his sister took the boy and gave him to Pharaoh's daughter, who took a liking to Jochebed's daughter and asked, "What is your name?" "Miriam," she replied. She was told she could come and play with the boy, and she did, there at the palace. She made up a song that she taught to Moses, who loved circle dancing. "Little boy in a basket, on, not in the river," they sang. "Godde weaves big dreams for little boys in baskets."

Moses grew up with Pharaoh's daughter, who raised him as her son. She eventually married and gave birth to a daughter, and named her Bithia. The girl could recite by heart the tale of Moses among the rushes, and when she had a daughter of her own, she named her Miriam.

✧ The Cushite Woman

Moses learned about Hebrew culture from his sister Miriam. She told him who he really was and provided a link to their mother and the world he had left behind. His roots were in two cultures, but in all external things he was thoroughly Egyptian.

When he was old enough to notice, Moses observed the many beautiful females in Pharaoh's palace. There were women from every culture. Some were slaves or servants or maids; others were personal attendants; still others, concubines. As a male of the royal family, he was told he had power over them, and if he pleased, whenever he pleased, he could take any one of them to bed, except for Pharaoh's favorites. He was not inclined to do so. One day, however, a new arrival stole his heart away. She was the color of ebony, young, and very frightened. She said she was from Nubia, or Cush, in the lower river valley, near the source of the Nile. She was taken by the army as spoils in a raid. They despised her Ethiopian culture. They said they would make her a slave. Moses went to Pharaoh's daughter and asked if he might have her, not for concubine, but as wife. Marriage was out of the question, he was told, for reasons of culture and class, but he could have her if he wanted. He did. They lived together quietly in his quarters in the palace. Miriam knew and was the first to be told when the woman was with child.

Moses had gone for a walk one day beyond the confines of the palace and saw the extent of the suffering endured by the Hebrew people. They were building an extension, straining under enforced labor, sweat drenching their brows, when an Egyptian foreman, dissatisfied, began beating one of the workmen. Moses was horrified. He drew the foreman aside and proceeded to chastise him, when the foreman made some rude remark about the Cushite woman and Moses. Furious, Moses hit him. To his dismay the blow to the head was hard enough to kill the foreman. Moses looked around and, seeing that there was no one observing them, he buried him in the sand. The next day Moses went out again and saw two Hebrews fighting. When he intervened, saying they should not fight one another, they said, "And who made you judge over us, you who are an Egyptian. Would you kill us and bury us in the sand like you did to one of your own?" Moses was frightened and hurried away. What if Pharaoh hears? he worried. He will surely turn on me. He will suspect me of being a Hebrew, of leading a rebellion against him. Word did get to Pharaoh. His daughter, who had been mother to Moses, told him her father was in a rage and was angry enough to kill him. So Moses fled. He left Egypt in search of a place of refuge and entered Midian, which was outside Egyptian territory. He regretted leaving his Cushite woman and his child-to-be behind.

✧ Seven Sisters _____

Moses remained in the land of Midian, uncertain where to settle. He camped by a well and watched as the villagers came for water. Now a local priest had seven daughters who were shepherding his sheep, and they came to water their flock. They were filling the troughs when some ill-natured shepherds arrived and drove them away. Moses came and stood up for the women and he stayed to water their flock. When he asked who they were, the seven sisters said they were daughters of Jethro and that their mother had died.

When they returned to their father, he said to them, "You are back early today." "We were helped by a stranger, an Egyptian," they replied. "He chased away those bullies. He even watered our flock." "Where is he?" Jethro asked in dismay. "Why have you left him standing there? You should have brought him back with you." They returned to the well and found Moses, and he went home with them. He agreed to remain with Jethro to oversee his flock. Soon after, Moses was attracted to one of the seven sisters. He married Zipporah, who helped him forget he was a very long way from home.

✧ The Burning Bush

Now Moses was pasturing Jethro's flock out in the wilderness by Horeb, which is called the mountain of Sinai. There he had a vision. S/HE appeared to him as fire in a bush, for suddenly the bush burst into flame, yet it was not consumed. "How can this be?" he wondered, moving forward for a better look. A Voice from the bush called out to him, "Moses! Moses!" "Here I am," he responded. Then all at once he heard, "Do not come any closer. Remove the sandals from your feet. You are standing on holy ground." Terrified, Moses hid his face, afraid of seeing God. "I have seen the misery of your people, and I have heard their cry," S/HE said. "I am sending you to deliver them from their sufferings and their oppression. You will bring my children out of Egypt to a land of milk and honey. Go to Pharaoh

and say to him, 'Let my people go.'" Moses began to protest, saying, "Who am I to go to Pharaoh? Who am I to play the hero? How shall I lead my people who are slaves in a foreign land?" S/HE said, "I will be with you. I will protect you wherever you go." "What will I tell my people?" he asked. "If I come and say, 'The God of your ancestors sent me to you,' and they ask me, what is your name, what shall I say to them?" S/HE said to Moses: "I AM WHO I AM." There was silence for a moment, then: "Say, 'I AM has sent me to you.'" Then the Voice and the Vision were gone.

✧ Zipporah _____

Moses returned to Zipporah. He told her all that had happened to him, and he was very distressed. He tried to explain that he was not the one. He was not quick-witted like his sister Miriam, nor eloquent like his brother Aaron. "I am slow of speech and thick of tongue. I cannot rally a crowd. I am not a leader. Let God send someone else." Zipporah answered sharply. "Aaron can speak when there is need to speak, and Miriam can rally the people. Godde has given this charge to you, and not to anyone else." She did her best to encourage him and to strengthen his resolve. She performed a religious ritual with a snake on a staff and a chalk white mask and waited as Moses agonized over saying "Yes!" to God.

Then the Voice returned again in a dream, saying, "Moses, go back to Egypt, for all who were seeking your life are dead." Indeed, Pharaoh had died and a new king reigned in Egypt. So Moses went to his father-in-law and said, "Give me leave to go to Egypt. I must return to my family there, while they are still alive." "Go in peace," said Jethro.

Now Zipporah had given birth to a son soon after marrying Moses. He had named the baby Gershom, saying, "I am an alien in a foreign land." She also had a second son, whom Moses named Eliezer, meaning, "God, my help, delivered me from the sword of Pharaoh." Moses took Zipporah and their two little sons, and they rode beside him on a donkey as he journeyed back to Egypt. On the way, at a place where they had stopped for the night, Moses was overcome with misgiving. "How can I lead the Hebrews," he said, "for I am not fully a Hebrew." He had never been circumcised. "And if I do not pay heed to God, then I shall surely die." He was so consumed with doubt and fear over not being circumcised, he did not know what to do. When at last he fell into a troubled sleep, Zipporah took a flint stone, and cut off her firstborn's foreskin. She carried the skin to Moses. Then she put her bloody hand between his legs and severed her husband's foreskin, chanting: "Bridegroom of blood. By circumcision, a bridegroom of blood. You are a bridegroom of blood to me." His pain was so intense, Moses was certain that he would die, but in a few days, he began to heal, and he came to this decision. Zipporah would return to her father's house and wait until he sent for her. Why bring a wife and children into a land from which one hopes to escape? So they parted, somewhat reluctantly, and Moses set out for Egypt.

❖ Miriam, Aaron, and Moses ⸻

As soon as Moses saw some of his people, he identified who he was, son of Jochebed and Aram, brother of Miriam and Aaron. Word spread quickly, and when Aaron heard, he went out into the wilderness to meet him. Moses told Aaron all that had happened, and he told it again to Miriam, for she too came out to him. Then Miriam assembled the elders of the people, and Aaron spoke to them all the words that God had given to Moses. The people believed and were overjoyed that God would relieve their misery and bring justice to the oppressed. They bowed to the ground in worship.

❖ The Cry of the Oppressed ⸻

Moses and Aaron went to Pharaoh to ask leave to go into the desert to give sacrifice to their God. All of their people had to go, a distance of three days' journey; those were the conditions set by God. "If we do not go, disease will strike, or we may fall beneath the sword." "I do not know this God," said Pharaoh. "I cannot let you go." He dismissed them and summoned the taskmasters and the supervisors of the Hebrews. "These slaves who may soon outnumber us are restless and discontent. They must not be allowed to be idle, for who knows what they might do?" So he gave them this command. "No more straw to make bricks. Let them go and gather their own straw, but do not decrease their quota. They must produce as they did before. They are lazy, which is why they say, 'Let us sacrifice to our God.' Give them more work, increase their burden, so there is no time to listen to those who would wish to lead them astray."

So the taskmasters and the supervisors carried out Pharaoh's orders. They told the workers, "No more straw. You will go and gather your own; and your quota will not be lessened." The people scattered everywhere, gathering stubble for straw to make bricks, and when they returned to complete their task, they could not achieve their quota. The taskmasters beat the Hebrew supervisors, saying: "Why did you come up short of bricks both today and yesterday? The amount is the same as before." The supervisors went before Pharaoh and cried, "Why do you treat your servants so? You withhold the straw and you say, 'Make bricks,' and when they can't, we are beaten." "Because you are lazy," Pharaoh replied. "Go back to work. Make bricks. As many as before." The supervisors left and were met by Moses and Aaron outside the palace. They said to the two, "Be gone from here. Look what you have done to us. You have caused a division between Pharaoh and us; we are a stench that reeks in his nostrils. You have given him means to kill us."

Then Moses cried out to God, saying, "Why have you chosen me for this task? Ever since I spoke to Pharaoh, it has been worse than it was before. You have done nothing to help me, you who promised to deliver my people." Then Moses heard the word of God: "Go tell Pharaoh to let my people go!" But Moses refused to be coerced. "My own people will not listen to me. Why should Pharaoh heed one as inarticulate as I?" Moses heard God's word to him, "I will be with you always," and he went out and wept.

✧ The Plagues _____

God spoke to Moses again, saying, "Pharaoh's heart is hardened." Then God told Moses to meet with Pharaoh, in the morning, by the river and say, "You have not listened to God's command to let my people go. Therefore, the waters of the Nile will reek and the river will be repugnant. It will be a sign that God is God, and a punishment to you."

Now the water of the Nile river was low due to a seasonal drought. The fish in the river began to die. The rushes died, then more fish died and littered the banks of the river. Meanwhile, the Hebrews in Goshen were going out to fish. Throughout the region they caught fish, from rivers and streams they gathered fish, but they did not keep their catch. Rather, under cover of darkness, they dumped the rotting carcasses along the banks of the Nile. The river reeked and the marshes stank. None could go to the Nile to bathe nor could they wash their garments, so even the people began to smell, and Pharaoh himself was repugnant. His courtesans dug in the sand by the river to find fresh drinking water, for they could not drink river water. Pharaoh was seething with anger. These people were a stench in his nostrils, but his heart was even more hardened, and he would not let them go.

Suddenly, the Hebrews were inspired. They had found a way to vex their oppressors. Yes, God had heard their cry. They decided next upon a plague of frogs, for these seemed plentiful. They caught frogs, thousands of frogs, every man, woman, and child caught frogs. They put them in bags and kept them alive.

Then under cover of darkness, they released the frogs in Pharaoh's palace. It was overrun with frogs. The court, courtyard, kitchens, chambers, even the beds and the kneading bowls, the ovens and bags of grain, everywhere, the palace was hopping with frogs. Pharaoh sent for Moses and said, "Remove these frogs and you may go and sacrifice to your God." "When may we go?" Moses asked. "Tomorrow," Pharaoh replied. That night, no one knows exactly how, the frogs departed the palace, but Pharaoh suddenly changed his mind, and the people could not go.

Then God inspired Moses. Unleash a plague of flies, said Moses, conspiring with the elders. So under cover of darkness, and inconspicuously during the day, the Hebrews dropped little bits of garbage and fragments of slaughtered carcasses and remnants of leftover food all around Pharaoh's palace, and here and there inside. The bits were so small that no one noticed, but everyone saw the flies. Flies swarmed Pharaoh's quarters, the women's quarters, the gardens, and all the officers' quarters, and seemed to multiply. They followed the cooks, invaded the cupboards, and ruined every meal. Pharaoh summoned Moses and said, "Go, sacrifice to your God, but do not cross the border." "We must go three days' journey into the wilderness," said Moses, "to do as God commands." "Do not go very far," said Pharaoh, adding, "intercede on my behalf." The flies disappeared, we know not how, but Pharaoh did not keep his word. The Hebrews did not go.

The people were disheartened. They did not know what else to do, for every time God made a way, Pharaoh denied them passage. So the people prayed, and God heard. That night there was a freak storm as sometimes occurs in the desert, only this time, thunder and lightning and hail lashed across the landscape, destroying gardens, felling trees and livestock left out in the open. Hail the size of olives and figs fell in heaps in the city and beyond. Lightning flashed and thunder cracked with a fury never seen before and never to be seen again. When the storm had finally abated, Pharaoh sent for Moses and said, "Enough

of your God's thundering anger. You and your people may go."
This time, he said, he meant it, but when he had taken time
to reflect, once again his heart hardened, and he would not let
them go.

The Hebrew people continued to hope long after the damage
had been repaired and life had returned to normal, but theirs
was not a normal life, and they prayed to be delivered. Just when
their hearts had begun to doubt, a cloud formed on the horizon,
thick and black and exceedingly wide. It moved forward with a
terrifying sound. Suddenly a dense swarm of locusts the likes of
which had never been seen, so big were they and so many, descended upon the grain to ensure it would never see a harvest.
They devoured everything in sight. All that had survived the
hailstorm fell to this voracious plague. Flowers, fruit, vegetation
disappeared and plants were reduced to stubble. There was no
green leaf remaining, nor a single kernel of grain. The locusts
moved on to the cities and towns. They swarmed into the palace
and covered all the surfaces, seeking something to devour. Pharaoh sent for Moses and pleaded, "Remove this hideous blight,
and go." Later he said to his chief officials, "These people, they
swarm all over me, and a deadly force is with them." However,
once the plague had passed, he refused to let them go.

The locusts were followed by other clouds, thick and gray,
with a tinge of black. As in myths of storm gods and other such
tales, a thick fog fell to earth and blotted out the sun, the sign of
Re, the sun god. For the only time in memory, the sun did not
rise for a week of days and darkness covered the land. Nights
without stars and days without sunlight depressed and frightened many, who wondered what these portents might mean,
and how many more disasters they might have to endure. Pharaoh summoned Moses and said, "Enough of this. Restore the
light. Then you and your people may go." Moses left. That night
he prayed, all the people prayed, and dawn returned with a daz-
zling brightness. Even so, Pharaoh recanted, and he would not
let them go.

The Hebrews observed their spring rite, the seasonal festival of newborn lambs, and prayed for their liberation. Moses said to the people, "Take the blood of the sacrificed lamb and spread it on the lintel and the doorposts of your house. When God's avenging angel comes wielding a sword of justice, this mark shall be a sign signifying God's beloved dwell therein, and death will pass you by." So they marked their houses, as Moses had said, and awaited the judgment of God.

For whatever reason, for the cause is unknown, although to believers it was clearly due to God's vindication, a deadly plague broke out in Egypt, claiming young and old. People cried out in fear and pain as the death toll mounted. Very few families were spared, except in the land of Goshen where the Hebrews, safe within their homes, avoided contact with the affected, while thanking and praising God. Death claimed Pharaoh's firstborn, an officer, and several slaves. Then a cry awakened him at midnight, and when he heard that his grandson had died, he summoned Moses and Aaron and said, "Get out of my land. Get out of my sight. Go now and sacrifice to your God. Deliver us from this evil curse, and ask a blessing on me."

So Moses and Aaron ran from Pharaoh to summon all their people. They knew they had to leave at once, before Pharaoh could change his mind.

✧ The Exodus

While Moses and Aaron had been plaguing Pharaoh, Miriam was meeting with the women and organizing their departure. They had decided to form small companies, each consisting of women and children, the elderly, and the infirm. Quietly and inconspicuously, they would slip out of Egypt, they said, over a period of several weeks, a company at a time. They would begin at once, no matter what Pharaoh decided. Their plan was to leave late in the evening and to travel through the night. They would go by way of Migdol, which meant heading toward the sea. They agreed to meet at a certain place where they would set up a temporary camp and await their menfolk there.

Trusted Egyptians knew of their plans. Many were sympathetic. They befriended the Hebrews and abhorred their mistreatment by tyrants none could control. Most Hebrew women and many men knew Egyptians to be kind and generous people and were careful not to confuse the many with the few demonic individuals who abused their positions of power.

So the women went to their neighbors and friends and asked for their assistance. The generosity of ordinary Egyptians made possible their escape. Women gave their jewelry to be sold or bartered for shelter and food, along with silver and gold. They said, "Here, take our clothing. Cover yourselves with these robes and veils so you will look like us, and you will pass as Egyptians." So the companies gathered, one at a time, disguised themselves as local people, and left under cover of darkness on nights when there was no moon. They took enough food for the initial journey and then bought or bartered for what they needed from nomads along the way. One by one the companies arrived at the meeting place near Migdol and added other tents. By the time locusts had descended on Pharaoh, nearly all the women had gone, taking with them the children, the elderly, and those who were infirm.

Without the children, the men were free to move with the speed of an arrow. They would have to be swift, for at any moment the army might come in pursuit. Moses and Aaron ran to Goshen when Pharaoh gave the order. Oh, what a night to remember! They mustered the men, along with the handful of women still remaining, and quickly prepared to depart. There was no need for disguises now. It was time to step forward, time to run. They took their bread before it was leavened, and with only the bare essentials in hand retraced the route the others had taken and caught up with them in Migdol. They took a brief rest, but that was all, for it was too soon for rejoicing. Pharaoh had changed his mind before. He would probably change it again.

Pharaoh indeed had a change of heart. "Why are we letting them leave our service? Who else will do what they do?" he said and charged his chariots of military men to pursue the departing Hebrews and bring them back in chains. They drove the horses hard, for the fugitives had a three-day advantage, yet what did that matter when the hunters' prey were trying to escape on foot. At last the soldiers caught sight of them, this side of the Sea of Reeds.

They were leaving Egypt by a roundabout way, up through the northern wilderness that was bordered by the sea. A clear path was ahead of them, except for some treacherous marshes along a coastal inlet that was known as the Sea of Reeds. Their Egyptian friends had warned them of this and had told them how they might cross over safely without getting caught in the mud. If the rains were late, it might be dry, but they still had to pass with caution. The waters there were never deep, but the mud was thick and deadly. More than once a wagon had slipped and disappeared under the muck.

They were approaching the Sea of Reeds when they heard the thundering hoofbeats. Turning, they saw an enormous regiment of soldiers descending upon them, their faces fierce, their swords upraised, their horses wet with foam. They looked ahead to the Sea of Reeds and their spirits sank within them, for the patchwork of water and mud and reed was dizzying to the eye. Where would they find safe footing? What if they slipped and got stuck in the mud? Why did God lead them out of Egypt only to see them die? "Here," shouted Miriam, "follow me," and she set out, leading the way. They followed her safely across the marsh and were so intent they failed to notice a strong west wind was rising. Clouds had gathered, lightning flashed, and just as the last of them cleared the marsh, a cloudburst covered the way they had come, leaving the mud under water. As quickly as the storm had arisen, just as quickly, it was gone. The chariots reached the edge of the marsh and did not pause for a moment. They knew the water was shallow there and posed no danger of drowning, so they plunged ahead and slammed to a halt, throwing every horse and every rider into a sea of reeds. The entire army was stuck in the mud and could pursue no further. No one knows how long it took them to climb free of the marshes, or if any at all had perished, or even if death by the Sea of Reeds would have been preferable to Pharaoh's wrath.

✦ Miriam's Song _____

Then Miriam took a tambourine and sang this victory song: "Sing to Godde for S/HE has led us safely through the sea." Over and over the people sang as she led them in the singing, adding verse upon verse expressing gratitude and praise. Many of the women joined with her to lead in the circle dancing, calling upon Shekinah to the beat of their tambourines.

The songs continued through the night and on into the morning, as they strove to put some distance between the oppressors and themselves. When it was safe to set up camp, they pitched their tents and rested, feeling free at last.

✦ Pillar of Cloud, Pillar of Fire _____

From that day forward, the people who had been delivered from death would be accompanied by a visible sign of S/HE who is always with them. By day a large cloud shielded them from the scorching desert sun, and by night stars in their constellations showed them which way to go.

The women marveled at so clear a sign of Shekinah's presence among them. "A pillar of cloud by day," they chanted, "a pillar of fire by night." In ritual and song they celebrated all that they knew and remembered of Godde, how S/HE Who Is had always been there in the tradition of past matriarchs and would surely guide them home. "I will be with you always," sang Miriam and the women, recalling the promise of S/HE Who Is, of Shekinah, of I AM.

As they sat in the evening under the stars, they spoke of S/HE Who Is as the I AM of Moses, of how they knew Godde in different ways, each by a different name. Elisheba, who was Aaron's wife and mother of his four sons, said, "This is what Godde is saying to us: 'I will be with you, as who I will be, will I be with you.'" For Elisheba, whose wisdom was honored by all, S/HE Who Is and I AM were one, and were present as Shekinah. The women marveled at these words. "The S/HE Who Is of women is the I AM WHO I AM of men," they sang, as they danced to their unfolding wisdom. They thought about this for many days, and their conversations continued through the months of desert nights.

✧ The Wilderness _____

They moved beyond the coastal region into the wilderness of Shur. Their pace was unhurried because of the children, the elderly, and the infirm. They had been walking for three days in the desert when they came upon a pool of water, but it was unfit to drink. Everyone was thirsty, and the children began to cry. A group confronted Moses. "What are we to drink?" they asked. Others started to grumble, but Moses prayed to God. Then Miriam came upon a branch of wood with fresh growth upon it. She knew it was a sign. So they pressed on, as complaints continued about the pool of water that they had named Marah, because of its bitterness. It may have been Moses who saw it first, an oasis on the horizon. Before nightfall, they came to Elim, where there were seventy palm trees and twelve springs of water. They camped there by the water, where they drank, washed, changed their garments, and praised a merciful God.

✧ Manna in the Wilderness ─────────────────

Once they left the oasis, they moved into the wilderness of Zin. It was hot and dry, with little to see, and food was hard to come by. Their daily rations dwindled. By the time they reached their next encampment, many were ready to leave. Some began to speak openly of what they had left behind. "Oh, for the flesh pots of Egypt," they said, "where we ate our fill of bread. You brought us into the wilderness only to die of hunger here." The women said, "Be patient," but too many days with too little to do and even less to eat and drink had made many men short-tempered. Moses and Aaron turned to prayer, while Miriam gathered the women. "Surely Godde did not bring us all this way, simply to leave us," she said. The women all agreed.

Now one of the women there in the camp was the Cushite slave of Pharaoh whom Moses had made his wife. On his last visit to Pharaoh's palace, he had slipped into the servants' quarters and searched until he had found her. He said, "I have come back for you." She and their little daughter managed to escape with the others that night. Moses carried his child as they ran, and when they arrived at Migdol, he put his wife and daughter into the care of his sister Miriam, and soon they were best of friends.

There in the wilderness of Zin reality hit with a deadening force. Hunger dominated daily routines. Nearly everyone was anxious. "How will we survive?" they asked, as fear spread through the tents. Then one evening a number of quails were sighted outside the camp. The men caught nearly all of them, and they feasted that night and the next. In the months ahead there would always be quail at least once every fortnight. Even when the birds no longer appeared, nomads knew where to find them.

One morning the ground was covered with a white sticky substance that looked like a layer of hoarfrost. Everyone was puzzled, except for the Cushite woman whom Moses had married. "We can eat the small white droplets," she said. "The substance is sweet and very good. In my country, it is a treat." So they gathered it up and ate their fill and referred to it as "manna," their bread of life in the wilderness, dropped from the hand of God. The Cushite explained to the women that their manna was really the droppings of insects that feed on the tamarisk tree. She did not tell this to the men. She also said they could eat the insect. There were times when some of them did. She taught the women many things about desert herbs and poultices. She was the one they turned to when any of them fell ill.

✧ Zipporah at Zin _____

Now Midian was near the wilderness of Zin, so Moses sent two messengers to Jethro and Zipporah, saying, "Tell my wife Zipporah, 'Moses sends for you.'" The messengers arrived after many days. Zipporah, her sisters, and their father were overjoyed to see them, and they listened to all that God had done for Moses and his people. Then Jethro saddled the camels and accompanied Zipporah and her sons to Moses, who had been waiting for them. When Moses saw them approaching, he hurried out to meet them, embraced his wife and children, and also his father-in-law, whom he held in high esteem. He took Zipporah into his tent and he spent the night with her, waiting until the morning to share with her that part of his life that was hard for him to tell. Because he loved Zipporah, it was with care and tenderness that he told her of his Cushite wife and of their little daughter. Zipporah accepted the news, for that was the way it was with men. Only Miriam would come to know just how much the news had hurt her.

Moses tried to convince Jethro to journey on with them. Jethro knew the desert well. He could lead them to food and water. He could choose the best and quickest routes to where they would be going. He was also a leader in his own right, and he was very wise. Jethro observed the ways of the camp, and then he went to Moses. He counseled Moses to get some help with the leadership of his people. "It is too much for one man," he said. "Let others resolve the petty disputes and mediate minor infractions. Give them something more to do and you will hear less complaining." So Moses did as Jethro advised. He selected a group of men and women to help in leading the people, along with Miriam and Aaron, who were already assisting him. Then Jethro said, "I must go now and return to my own country." No matter how hard he tried, Moses could not persuade Jethro to remain there with them.

✧ Springs of Living Water ⸻

They left the wilderness of Zin and journeyed south in stages, down to Rephidim. They were blessed with a daily supply of manna all along the way and had come to depend on it. The trees that offered occasional shade sheltered their food supply, but this was never certain. Awaiting it became a test of faith, since manna was only good for the day and could not be held over. Whenever anyone stored some up, it spoiled or rotted away.

They set up camp at Rephidim, for they were told there would be water, but there was none to be found. The people quarreled among themselves, and then they were angry with Moses. "Give us water to drink," they shouted. "Why bring us out of Egypt to kill us all with thirst?" Then Moses cried to God, saying, "What shall I do with these people? They are ready to stone me." Miriam approached her brother and said, "The local women say, use your stick. Over there, by the rock." So Moses went and struck the rock, but still there was no water. Miriam and Elisheba picked up sticks and began to dig in the sand. There, just below the surface, were springs of living water, cool and fresh from underground sources, sustaining for generations those who lived in this arid land. Moses named the place, calling it Massah and Meribah, because here the people had quarreled and had put God to the test, saying, "Is God among us or not?" Once again, God was with them.

✧ The Wilderness of Sinai ⸻

They did not stay long at Rephidim. The people were anxious to arrive somewhere, although they did not know where they were going. On the third new moon following their exodus from Egypt, they came into the Sinai and camped in the wilderness, in full view of the mountain. Moses went up the mountain to have a word with God.

While Moses was gone the men gathered to express their discontent. "What are we doing here?" they grumbled. "We left Egypt to be shepherds in Canaan, not to be desert nomads. All we do is wander around. Canaan is the other way." Many among them agreed. "Who is this God of Moses?" they asked. "And where might they be leading us?" The women began to worry. Some men talked of breaking ranks and heading out on their own. Others spoke of a new leader, someone more aggressive, someone capable of drawing his sword, who knew where the land of Canaan was and how to get there from here.

More frightening to the women was the growing consensus among the men to take Canaan by force. They all knew why they had not gone directly from Egypt to Canaan. The situation there had changed since the time of the ancestors. Land was no longer available to settle where one pleased. The whole of Canaan was occupied by various tribes and nations. How could a group the size of theirs just walk across the border without raising some alarm? They had talked about this for weeks, all the way from Zin to Rephidim. The women had always insisted, "We must enter Canaan peacefully. We must never resort to violence, nor spill one drop of blood." They had managed to prevent a move from the more militant among them, but now that seemed to be changing.

✧ Theophany on Mount Sinai

Meanwhile, Moses on the mountain top was hearing a word from God, who spoke to him of the covenant and of an everlasting love. He wept as he heard the eternal word ringing in his heart: "I bore you up on eagles' wings and brought you to myself." He knew that God was with him, that God would always be with him. How could he make them understand?

Moses returned to the people and asked them to pray and prepare themselves for an encounter with I AM. For three days all was well. The spirit in the camp was more subdued. Tensions eased. The bickering stopped. On the morning of the third day, everyone stood at the foot of the mountain in solidarity with Moses as he went up to meet with God. A cloud covered the mountain, for the glory of God was in the cloud and had deigned to sojourn there. Moses entered into the cloud and remained all day and through the night and through many nights and days. Mount Sinai was wrapped in a thick white cloud all the time he was there on the mountain. God spoke to Moses, and Moses prepared two tablets of stone. On these he affirmed the covenant, with words the finger of God had written on the tablets of his heart.

✧ The Golden Calf

When Moses did not return that day, the people merely wondered. After three days, they grew anxious. When a week had passed, someone said, "Perhaps he has died of hunger." Others said, "He has been consumed in the raging fire of God, for see there is smoke on the mountain." The mood soon turned to anger at having been abandoned, out there in the wilderness, with none on earth to guide them. Then suddenly it shifted, giving rise to new concerns. "Come," some said, "let us make an image of a god who will go before us. We need to take some action. Moses is gone, and for all we know, his god has gone with him." Many of the men agreed with this and prepared to construct an image of a god who would accompany them to Canaan. They would choose another leader in place of the absent Moses, and they would consecrate this leader when they met to worship god. The women all resisted. Gold was taken from a number of tents, whatever could be collected, for not everyone took part. Some men took the gold earrings of their sisters and wives and daughters, more often than not, by force. They melted these down, made a mold, and fashioned a golden calf.

As Moses came down from the mountain with the two tablets in his hands, he saw a crowd assembled there. They were just beginning a ritual dance before a golden calf. Moses was enraged. He smashed the tablets against a stone, took the calf and destroyed it, and castigated those responsible for leading the others astray. They made some attempt to defend themselves. "We needed an image of God for ourselves, something we could relate to. We do not know this I AM of yours. God must have a name." Then Moses said to the people, "YHWH is God's name," and he trembled as he said it. "YHWH said these words to me up there on the mountain: 'I am your God who brought you out of the land of Egypt, who delivered you from slavery. You shall have no other gods.'" Then Moses added his own words. "You are a stiff-necked people. Why should YHWH go with you into the land of Canaan? You turn against me, you turn against God, you turn against one another. Beware the wrath of YHWH." Cries of remorse arose from the crowd. In the days ahead, much time was spent in making restitution. The people begged Moses to return to the presence of God and intercede for them.

✧ The Tablets

In the stillness of evening, when all around was wrapped in a sacred silence, two of the women went to the place where Moses had smashed the tablets, and they picked up the broken shards. They met with some others outside the camp and pieced the stones together. Miriam studied the tablets, tracing the primitive characters in the silver-fingered moonlight. Slowly, she read the words aloud. "Love God with all your heart, and with all your soul, and with all your might." And from the second tablet she read: "Love your neighbor as yourself."

The women sat in silence. Many were moved to tears. "These

are words of wisdom," they said. "S/HE Who Is has revealed to Moses the wonderful ways of Godde." They wondered how they might live these words in a world so prone to waging war and plundering a neighbor. How could they convince their husbands to embrace a lasting covenant with the One Whose way is love? "We are not strong enough," they said. Then Elisheba proclaimed this oracle: " 'I will be with you, as who you need me to be, will I be with you.' Thus says Godde." Miriam spoke as a prophet would speak: "Godde is our Rock and our Refuge. Godde is our Strength and a Shield against the wiles and the wounds of the day." The women were strangely comforted. Sitting a distance from the camp where the shadow of Mount Sinai lay like a deep, dark pool of mystery casting its circle around them, the women sang softly into the night:

S/HE is my shepherd, I shall not want.
S/HE guides me to green pastures,
leads me beside still waters
where S/HE restores my soul.
I pass through the valley of danger and death without fear,
for S/HE is with me
and is quick to comfort me.
Surely goodness and mercy shall follow me
all the days of my life,
and I shall dwell with S/HE Who Is
forever and forever.

Before they slipped back into their tents, each of the women took a shard and promised to protect it. There could be a time in the days ahead when they would have to reassemble again.

With a slow step and a heavy heart, Moses climbed the mountain to intercede once more with God. "Forgive this sin," he pleaded. "Allow us to make amends." God said, "I forgive," and Moses felt transformed. "Show me your glory," Moses cried, for his innards burned like fire. Then the goodness of God passed through him and the glory of God passed over him as Moses hid in a cleft in a rock, so as not to look at God. "I will renew my covenant with the descendants of Jacob whose name is Israel," said God, and promised to accompany them to a land of milk and honey. Then Moses took two tablets of stone similar to the first ones, and he wrote down the commandments of the covenant with God.

✧ Departure from Sinai _____

When Moses came down from the mountain, his face was shining and serene and the people were amazed. "Israelites," he addressed them, "YHWH will go with us. We are leaving now for Canaan." The people burst into cheers as the call to go forward rang through the air. They broke camp and departed from the wilderness of Sinai with its rugged mountain ranges and retraced their steps northward through the wilderness of Paran. "Shekinah is with us," the women sang, as they camped for a while at the large green oasis of Paran. Indeed, God's Presence was with them, for the cloud continued to accompany them, and the fire was in the cloud. No dissension disturbed the peace. They were marching on to Canaan.

✧ Land of Milk and Honey

They set up camp at Kadesh-barnea at the southern tip of Canaan, near where the border crosses through the wilderness of Zin. Kadesh was an oasis. There were numerous springs in the region around it, so that water was never lacking. It was the perfect place from which to launch a military objective, should the need ever arise. This desert settlement marked a turning point for the Israelites in their journey, for there the people coalesced and became a single nation born of a common focus, to return to their ancestral land. Women fully supported the intent to enter the land of Canaan, but when men spoke of armed assault, they steadfastly dissented.

A small contingent of men was sent to spy on the land of Canaan and to return with a report. "Go up into the Negeb and continue on into the hills, and see what the land is like," they were told, "whether the people there are weak or strong, whether they are few or many, whether the land is good or bad, rich or poor, whether there are trees and the kinds of trees and the names of the fruits that grow there. Find out too whether the towns are unwalled or fortified." So the spies went forth, and for forty days they spied on the land of Canaan. They returned with a large cluster of grapes that two of them had carried on a pole all the way from Hebron, and some pomegranates and figs. This was the report they gave to all the Israelites who had assembled. "We entered the land to which we were sent. It flows with milk and honey, and here are some of its fruits. However, the inhabitants are fierce, and their towns are large and fortified. We cannot go up against these people, for they are stronger than we are." At that point, Caleb intervened. "Let us go in at once," he said, "and occupy the land. We can overcome any resistance." Others, however, objected. "The land that we spied upon devours its inhabitants. The people there are giants. We ourselves are like grasshoppers, and we will seem as such to them. They will easily crush us all."

Many who heard this were filled with fear, and they wept in despair and anger. "Would that we had died in Egypt! Or in the wilderness! Why has YHWH brought us here only to die by the sword? Our wives and children will be spoils of war. Let us go back to Egypt!" Then they conspired together, saying, "Let us put someone in charge of leading us back to the land of Egypt." The women said, "We will not go. We will not go back to Egypt, nor can we go forward with blood on our hands. We will stay here in the desert." The whole camp was divided. They had not experienced such despair since searching for straw for their quota of bricks, and the thought of making more bricks for Pharaoh was even more alarming. Joshua, who had been a spy in the land, joined with Caleb to try to restore some unity among the people. He said, "The land we saw is prime land. YHWH will bring us into this land that is flowing with milk and honey. We need not fear the people there, for if God is truly on our side, than who can be against us?" He was not very convincing, for they rose up and threatened to stone him. It took many days and long conversations to calm the people enough to consider the choices that lay before them. Egypt was out of the question. That meant that either they entered Canaan or they remained in the desert where they and their children's children would be nomads all their lives. So it was that they decided to go forward into Canaan, although the camp remained divided on how they would meet their objective, or even if it could be met.

✧ Foreign Women, Foreign Gods

It was agreed that any plan of action required more information. Perhaps a second look at the land along its eastern border might reveal some way of peaceful entry and eliminate the necessity of moving ahead by force. So a large contingent of Israelites went up into the wilderness of Moab to learn about the land.

Now the Moabites had heard that a Hebrew force was amassing in the wilderness of Zin, and they were very afraid. When they saw a contingent there in their midst, camped in the plains of Moab not far from the river Jordan in sight of Jericho, their hearts were filled with dread. They said to their Midianite neighbors, "This horde has come to devour us as the ox devours the grass." The king of Moab set out to put a curse on the Israelites. For this he hired Balaam the seer, but God touched the heart of the diviner, saying, "Do not curse these people," and when Balaam opened his mouth to speak, blessings came forth. Word of this spread far and wide. Some said of Balaam, "What a donkey, that man! Stubborn as a mule! He lost a reward of silver and gold. He cursed himself with a blessing." Others were amazed at his oracles. "So great is his power," they said, "even his donkey prophesied!"

While encamped at Shittim, a number of Israelite men became involved with the women of Moab and entered into relationships that were physical and even religious. They joined the women for sacrificial meals and brought them back to the camp at night. When the camp's leaders returned from a foray into Canaan, they were furious and said, "When Moses hears, he will kill us all. Cut off from these women and their foreign gods, lest every one of us die." So the men sent the women away, all the men but Zimri, a Simeonite and son of the highly respected Salu. He had fallen in love with a Midianite woman whom he was determined to marry. The woman's name was Cozbi. Her mother, Zur, was descended from an ancestral house in Midian and was matriarchal head of a clan. Despite the threats and protests, Zimri took Cozbi to his tent and he made her his wife. She agreed to remain with him and to live among his people, and they received a blessing from Zur.

The time came to break camp and return to Kadesh-barnea in the wilderness of Zin, where a report was made to Moses in the presence of all the people. The group's captain told of how they had mixed with local women, that many had slept with them, had even sacrificed to their gods. Moses was furious. "Lest God's anger be against us, shall we not take those who have sinned and impale them in the sun?" Everyone was stunned. Moses continued, "YHWH forbids other gods. I command you to avoid foreign gods by avoiding foreign women. Who takes a foreign woman to bed or keeps her as his wife shall be cut off from Israel and no longer be one of us." The whole camp fell silent. Just then Zimri appeared. He stood before Moses and all the people, and with him was the Midianite woman he had brought home to his family. Several of the elders protested, for their anger was enkindled. When Zimri saw their hostility, he took Cozbi by the hand and led her into his tent. Phinehas, Elisheba's grandson who was also the grandson of Aaron the priest, got up and left the assembly. Before anyone could stop him, he took a spear, followed Zimri and Cozbi into their tent, and stabbed them both to death. A wail went up from the women when they saw what had been done. Elisheba mourned the victims, even as her heart bled for the child of the child of her womb. Shelomith, daughter of Dibri and a member of the tribe of Dan, raised her voice from the crowd and prayed: "Godde, forgive the guilt of us all, for this blood is on our hands." An Israelite began to challenge her, accusing her of giving birth to the son of a foreigner, for Shelomith had married an Egyptian. Her son rose up to defend her, and he and the other got into a fight before Moses and all the people. The one who had started the trouble stopped, as if the fight were over, then he picked up a rock and brought it down on the head of Shelomith's son. "A curse on you!" he said, after he had stoned the boy to death. There was chaos at Kadesh-barnea and anger as had never before been seen throughout their wilderness wandering.

✧ Miriam Challenges Moses _____

Miriam stood up in the midst of the people and challenged the authority of Moses to do as he had commanded. She said he did not understand the religious ways of women. She said that women worshiped one Godde, whom sometimes they called Asherah, or Anat, or Shekinah, or Shaddai. YHWH, she said, was another name that God had revealed to Moses and to the patriarchs before him, while Shekinah was the presence of Godde experienced by women. She asked, "Has S/HE spoken only through Moses? Has S/HE not spoken also through us?" Then Miriam questioned his decision regarding foreign women. Had he not married Zipporah? Was she not a Midianite, the daughter of a Midianite priest? And what of the Cushite woman he had married, for indeed he had married a Cushite. "Will you send your wives away?" she asked. "If not, then how can you forbid others to marry outside the tribe?" For the second time, the assembly was stunned and could not utter a word.

Aaron defended his sister and added these words of his own. "Fear breeds hatred, and hatred leads to violence. How can it be that we have allowed injustice to dominate? We were once slaves in Egypt. Have we forgotten already how we were unjustly treated because of our different ways? Would we now oppress others with a similar contempt? Mistreatment of those different from us has led to more than one death this day. Parents have lost their children, and my son no longer knows his son." Then Miriam told Moses she could not obey his orders. She would be moving outside the camp. She would not go to Canaan with them.

So Miriam moved out of the camp. She set her tent some lengths away, and all the men avoided her as though she were unclean or afflicted with leprosy. Only a day or so had passed before the women joined her. They left their husbands and older sons and set up their tents near Miriam's tent, determined to remain with her. They wept because of the violence that had spread like a plague among them, and they mourned the decision of their men to invade the land of Canaan and to kill if they went to war. "Our sons will follow their fathers," they cried. "The child of our womb will slaughter the child of another woman's womb. May Godde have mercy on us, for S/HE is Mother of all."

The women talked a lot about Canaan and wondered, was it worth it, for how could they ever enjoy possessing something taken by force? They said, "Milk and honey, Godde's bounty, flow freely from a Mother's breast to nourish all the children, never favoring one child to the detriment of the rest." And then, "A land of milk and honey must be a land where women flourish and are free to offer milk and honey rituals to Godde." The wisdom of the women flowed as encouragement and comfort. It was for them both milk and honey in a spiritual wilderness.

Moses, meanwhile, turned to Godde, for his sister's words had wounded and his heart was sore distressed. "Why am I in disfavor?" he cried. "Why have you laid the burden of these stiff-necked ones on me? Have I conceived these people? Did I give birth to them? Then why is it you say to me, 'Carry them in your bosom, as a mother carries a nursing child,' to a land of milk and honey? Well, I cannot carry them any longer, for they are too heavy for me." Deeply discouraged, he shouted to God: "If this is the way you would treat me, then put me to death at once." Moses struggled with doubt and despair, for God was slow in lifting a hand to remove his misery. When God at last appeared to Moses, the words came in a dream. "There are prophets here among you. I make myself known to them in visions. I speak to them in dreams."

For seven days Miriam sat in her tent outside the camp, and the women were there with her. Then Moses came to Miriam and said, "You were with me by the water when I was but a child and you delivered me from death. You crossed over the waters with me as leader of the people and delivered us all from death. Time after time you have led us to an oasis in the desert. You give the water of life to me from the wellspring of your wisdom. Let us find a way, you and I, to go forward again together."

So Miriam and Moses reconciled, although there were a number of things Moses never did understand. That day Miriam and Aaron and Moses vowed they would not cross into Canaan if it meant the shedding of blood. "Even if others do so, we will not cross the threshold," they said, "unless we go in peace." When Miriam was brought back into the camp, all the women folded their tents and were reconciled to their families. Not a single plan had been put forward until Miriam had been brought in again.

There was a period of relative peace as the leadership struggled to honor the wishes of the women. Then on the night of the new moon, barely a year after arriving at the oasis of Kadesh, Miriam died and was buried there, near a spring of running water. For many days and many nights, there was no water to nourish the people, for their wellspring of wisdom was gone.

✧ Daughters of Zelophehad ─────────

During those days at Kadesh-barnea, Moses and the elders were completing the statutes and ordinances that would define the Israelites. These were the laws that would order their lives as a people in the land of Canaan. Part of the task involved determining the amount of land to be allotted to each of the clans and their families once they were in Canaan. What had become clear in the process was how much the patriarch's influence, which placed sons over daughters and favored the firstborn son, dominated everywhere.

Zelophehad was of Manasseh's clan. His lineage went back to Joseph, through Hepher and Gilead and Machir, to Manasseh, who was Joseph's son. Zelophehad would not be entering Canaan, for he died in Kadesh-barnea and was buried there in the desert. Now Zelophehad had no sons, but he had five feisty daughters. The name of the eldest was Mahlah; then came Hoglah, Milcah, and Tirzah. The youngest girl was Noah.

One day the daughters of Zelophehad came to Moses and the elders and said, "Our father died in the wilderness without leaving sons. Why should his name be removed from his clan because he has had no son? Give us an inheritance among our father's brothers." So Moses withdrew to consider. He decided to present their case to God, and this is the answer God gave him: "Let the daughters inherit, for they have a legitimate point." So Moses wrote into law these words, "If a man dies and has no son, then his daughter shall inherit. This shall be for the Israelites a statute and ordinance, for so has God revealed it." For a week of nights the women danced, celebrating the sisters, for in every generation now, their daughters would inherit.

✧ Noah _____

Mahlah and her sisters were leaders among the women after Miriam died. The older girls were high-spirited. Noah was more serene. Noah was the keeper of memories, they said, for indeed she would tell the stories of the matriarchs and their daughters, weaving into the narratives her own intuitive wisdom to be kept and handed on. Noah heard the spirits, they said. Noah sang their songs.

Noah's mother and grandmother had introduced her as a little girl to the ritual ways of women. Her spirit was shaped by the rhythms of the sacred in all seasons; her heart beat in harmony with the cosmic pulse of life. Noah loved rainbows and had no fear of water, even though she had seen the floodwaters of the Nile overflow its banks. Time and again, her sisters would find her dancing in the rain.

Noah, like her namesake who had conquered the waters of destruction to embrace a new beginning, had made a covenant with S/HE Who Is. She vowed she too would honor and protect all that had life around her, for Noah believed with all her heart that earth was the lovesong of Godde.

Through all the hard times leading up to the exodus from Egypt, Noah never doubted that Godde would one day deliver her from all her captivities, for she knew, as a woman, there were many ways a person might be bound. Both her mother and her grandmother died before the run for freedom, yet Noah knew, wherever she was, that they would be there with her.

The wilderness was, for Noah, oasis for the spirit. She knew that Shekinah, Who was all around her and present deep within her, had lured her into the wilderness in order to speak to her heart. On nights when the moon was full in the sky, the women would hear Noah singing:

S/HE Who Is, Shaddai, Shalom,
hone our spirits,
lead us home.
Shekinah, mother of all living things,
shelter us beneath Your wings,
shelter us
beneath your wings.

Then Noah would open her cloth bundle and finger the keep-sakes cradled there: a shard from a broken tablet, a black stone from a sea of reeds, a chip of brick made out of straw, and some things her mother had given her the day before she died. She had said that the small clay figurine that had the color and feel of earth and the handful of encrusted shells were ancient *teraphim* that had come from her great grandmother, who could not remember whose they were or the path that they had taken. During her rituals and her silent prayer, Noah would hold them close and smile, perhaps because she knew.

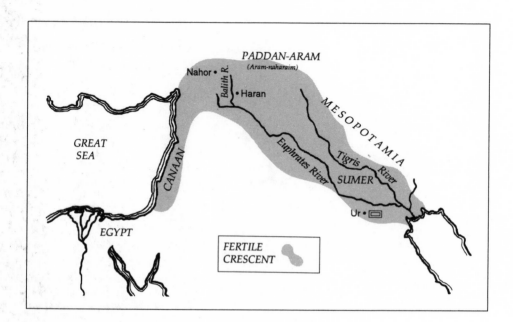

Map of the Journey
through Genesis and Exodus

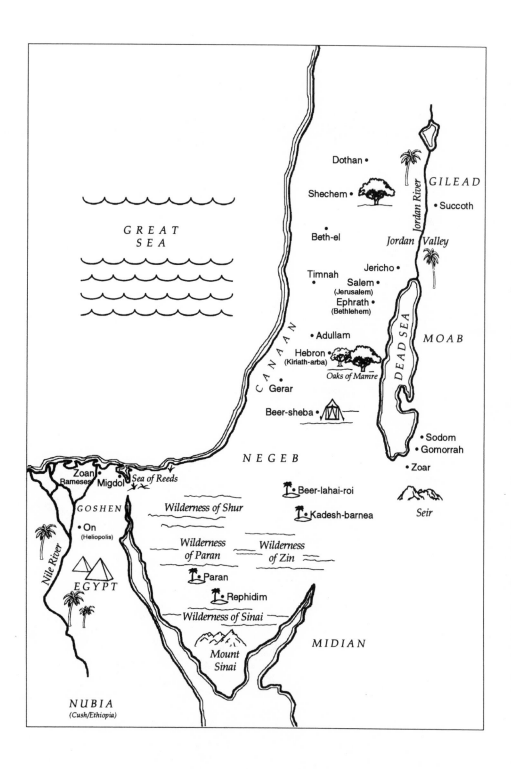

WomanWisdom
A Feminist Lectionary and Psalter
Women of the Hebrew Scriptures: Part I

Celebrations of women of the Hebrew Scriptures, including readings, psalms, and prayers for worship services and biographical information.

Illus. 352pp. 0-8245-1100-X pb $16.95

WomanWitness
A Feminist Lectionary and Psalter
Women of the Hebrew Scriptures: Part II

More readings, psalms, and prayers, with a comprehensive index of all the women in the Bible, as featured in the trilogy of books: *WomanWord, WomanWisdom, WomanWitness.*

Illus. 352pp. 0-8245-1141-7 pb $16.95

WomanPrayer, WomanSong
Resources for Ritual

Ritual and song that capture feminine biblical images of God, provide feminine God language, and introduce us to our foremothers.

254pp. 0-8245-1025-9 pb $16.95

Please ask for these titles at your bookstore or to order direct send payment (including $3.00 for the first book and $1.00 for each additional book to cover shipping and handling fees) to Crossroad, 370 Lexington Avenue, New York, NY 10017.

OTHER PUBLICATIONS
BY THE AUTHOR

Books

Preparing the Way of the Lord
God-With-Us: Resources for Prayer and Praise
Why Sing? Toward a Theology of Catholic Church Music
An Anthology of Scripture Songs
WomanPrayer, WomanSong: Resources for Ritual
WomanWord: Women of the New Testament
WomanWisdom: Women of the Hebrew Scriptures: Part One
WomanWitness: Women of the Hebrew Scriptures: Part Two
The Gospel According to Mary: A New Testament for Women

Records/Cassettes/Published Music Collections

Joy is Like the Rain
I Know the Secret
Knock, Knock
Seasons
Gold, Incense, and Myrrh
In Love
Mass of a Pilgrim People
RSVP: Let Us Pray
Songs of Promise
Sandstone
Remember Me
WomanSong
EarthSong

Music resources are available from
Medical Mission Sisters
77 Sherman Street, Hartford, CT 06105
203–233–0875/203–232–4451